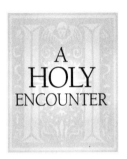

A
HOLY
ENCOUNTER

Meeting God in His Word

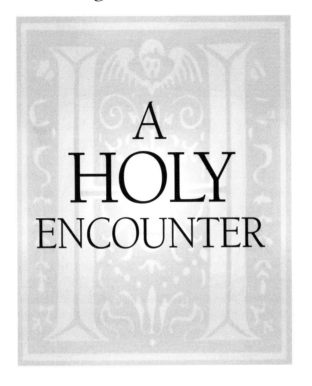

A
HOLY
ENCOUNTER

CARL M. LETH

Beacon Hill Press of Kansas City
Kansas City, Missouri

Copyright 1998
by Beacon Hill Press of Kansas City

ISBN 083-411-6332

Printed in the
United States of America

Cover Design: Kevin Williamson

All Scripture quotations not otherwise designated are from the *Holy Bible, New International Version*® (NIV®). Copyright © 1973, 1978, 1984 by International Bible Society. Used by permission of Zondervan Publishing House. All rights reserved.

Permission to quote from other copyrighted versions of the Bible is acknowledged with appreciation:

The *Revised Standard Version* (RSV) of the Bible, copyright 1946, 1952, 1971 by the Division of Christian Education of the National Council of the Churches of Christ in the USA.

The Living Bible (TLB), © 1971. Used by permission of Tyndale House Publishers, Inc., Wheaton, IL 60189. All rights reserved.

Scripture quotations marked KJV are from the King James Version.

Library of Congress Cataloging-in-Publication Data
Leth, Carl M.
 A holy encounter : meeting God in his Word / Carl M. Leth.
  p. cm.
 ISBN 0-8341-1633-2 (pbk.)
 1. Bible—Theology—Prayer-books and devotions—English. 2. Word of God (Theology)—Prayer-books and devotions—English. 3. God—Worship and love—Prayer-books and devotions—English. I. Title.
BS543.L48 1998
242'.5—dc21   97-45876
                                                                   CIP

10 9 8 7 6 5 4 3 2 1

CONTENTS

INTRODUCTION

This series of devotional studies has three purposes. Encountering God through the Scriptures is the starting point for all three. In His Word God reveals himself to us. He also reveals us to ourselves. Through Scripture we reach toward our first purpose: *understanding.* The second purpose, *worship,* is the natural response to our understanding of God and His will for us. Seeing God, knowing Him more truly, we are moved to worship Him. Our third purpose, *practical discipleship,* is also a result. In knowing God we are moved to love Him, and we are enabled and empowered to live for Him.

Expressed another way, we might understand this volume as a devotional introduction to biblical theology. Biblical theology is, after all, the knowledge of God as we find it expressed in Scripture. It need not be dry and obscure. In fact, it is the doorway through which we enter to meet God.

Geoffrey Wainwright, in his *Doxology,* first helped me to understand how theology, worship, and life are linked together. Seen in this way, seeking to understand God is actually a form of worship. By coming to an understanding, we are moved to an attitude of devotion. Genuine encounter with God prompts a response of service and discipleship. This response is shaped and directed by a deeper understanding of God that matures and focuses our discipleship.

In this devotional study we will focus on a biblical theme, character, or book each week. Each study has six lessons. Sunday will be considered a time of worship as well as reflection on and response to the material from the week.

1

CREATION AND FALL

INTRODUCTION

This week we look at the beginning of time. We find some lessons about who God is and what He is about. We see what we as humans could have been and can still hope to be. And we see what sin is. In Genesis, God's creation and sin's effects are graphically portrayed so that we clearly see the options before us. The story of creation and the Fall is more than a history of the distant past. It is a reality that takes place today in our lives and in our world.

QUESTIONS TO THINK ABOUT

What does Gen. 1—4 tell us
    about God?
    about man (male and female)?
    about the effect of sin on us?
    about the effect of sin on the world?
    about the effect of sin on our society?
What is the contrast presented in Gen. 1—4?
What does Gen. 1—4 say to me in my life?

CREATION AND FALL—*Gen. 1:1-25*

In the beginning God created the heavens
and the earth (Gen. 1:1).

All too often this passage is a source of controversy and strife about the method of creation. We rush past the first verse to the proofs and arguments we find in those that follow. But the rest merely amplify and explain the deep truth of verse 1. The creation story in Genesis is trying to tell us something important—that in the beginning, before the world, the moon and stars, or *anything,* our God *was.* Jesus said He *is.* We can look before the beginning of time and find Him—our God—just as we will find Him beyond the end of time. All creation comes from Him and moves toward Him. And He is *our* God.

In the unknowable before time, He purposes to act in creation. Surely He knew what the price would be. Yet He chose to create in love and gracious providence. We have studied only one verse of the Bible, yet He has shown us already what He is and how we may know Him. Look at the world around us. Even in its brokenness, it is overwhelming to see the wonder and power and loving care He has portrayed in creation. And it was all for us. God didn't need us. He wasn't lonely. He was loving, and His love caused Him to create us and the miracle of creation in which we live.

Did He do it in six 24-hour days? Does it matter? God is God, and He could create as surely in a millennium as in a moment. When we insist that He act in ways that we recognize as miraculous, we try to make God in our own image. God could have made all of creation in six days, but the miracle is that "in the beginning God created." Not chance. Not fate. Not a disinterested deity. God, who shows His love and care in His work, created this world and the universe that surrounds it—because He loves us.

THOUGHTS BEFORE GOD:

Father, I stand in awe before all You have created. But more than for the objects of creation, I thank You for showing us what You are through Your creation. Help me allow Your creative love to work in me and through me today.

CREATION AND FALL—*Gen. 1:26—2:3*

So God created man in his own image,
in the image of God he created him;
male and female he created them (Gen. 1:27).

Man (male and female) was created as the pinnacle of God's creation and in His own image. We are special people. God made all of creation and gave it to us that we might be stewards of it and that it might serve us. We are inheritors together of the riches of God's creation. As His children we should be free to enjoy creation in a special way. As Christians we should live in a conscious awareness that it is given to us—by our Father.

This is my Father's world.
He shines in all that's fair.
In the rustling grass I hear Him pass;
He speaks to me ev'rywhere.
                              —Maltbie D. Babcock

It also means that *we* are His creation—in His image. Our humanness is not something to escape or conquer. We battle sin, but in winning that battle we become truly human rather than something other than human. Somehow we have come to regard "spiritual" activities and vocations as superior to "earthly" ones. But if Adam had not sinned, he would have been a farmer and animal caretaker. The "spiritual" vocations are a corrective to a world fallen in sin. They are truly necessary but not superior to the person who cares for plants or animals as a conscious steward of God's creation. God does not attempt in Christ to free us *from* being human but to free us *to be* truly human—in His image.

THOUGHTS BEFORE GOD:

What a special privilege to be created in Your image! You created me as someone and something very special. Help me see myself and this world as a special gift from You—given in love.

✦ CREATION AND FALL—*Gen. 2:15-17; 3:1-7*

For God knows that when you eat of it
your eyes will be opened, and
you will be like God, knowing good and evil (Gen. 3:5).

Oh, Adam and Eve, how could you sacrifice all that God offered in exchange for a taste of forbidden fruit? We cannot comprehend how great was the fall of man and woman. Imagine a world of peace, free of disease and struggle, and offering fellowship with God himself. All of that was sacrificed in a moment. Yet how can we accuse Adam and Eve? Haven't we each freely turned from the garden to eat of the tree forbidden to us?

Why do we do it? Because we want to be God. We decide that we can do better ourselves than God has done. Or at our worst, we decide that we would rather be a lord in hell than a servant in heaven. Oh, foolish person, it is not given to you to be lord of all! Eve was not exercising her independence, but her service to Satan. And this is sin; we love ourselves and desire to be lords of our own lives. All sins proceed from this.

Eve did not trust God to do what was best for her. She doubted His goodwill toward her. So she enthroned herself, and Adam followed. They rejected being the obedient servants of God (and masters of creation for Him) and became lords of themselves (and slaves to sin). How foolish they seem! Yet how like us they are! Sin is a lifestyle of loss and bondage chosen in preference to a lifestyle of wholeness and freedom.

✦ THOUGHTS BEFORE GOD:

Father, help me not to doubt You. Protect me from my own pride and selfishness. I know Your will is best for me. Help me be content with that.

CREATION AND FALL—*Gen. 3:8-13*

And they hid from the LORD God
among the trees of the garden (Gen. 3:8).

Humanity has been hiding ever since Adam and Eve ate the forbidden fruit. It is in the nature of sin to want to be hidden. Rather than face our sins and turn to God, we choose, incredibly, to try to hide from Him. Watch how sin operates in the lives of those around you. Although it is sin itself that brings us to misery, we are driven to seek sin—and its misery—even more desperately in an attempt to cure the sickness that it brings with it. We see this principle in the alcoholic or drug user who must use even more of his or her drug to escape the consequences, the emptiness or sickness, that the drug brought in the first place. The person who is disenchanted with casual sexual relationships seeks even more illusory relations. The person who is disillusioned by wealth or material possessions seeks them more frantically. We are truly twisted by sin—so twisted that we mistake the cause for the cure.

Even when faced by God, Adam still attempted to hide behind Eve, and Eve behind the serpent. We will go to any lengths rather than admit we are wrong. Pride cannot and will not confess, "I am wrong and I have failed as lord of my own life." This is the tragedy of sin. It leads us toward death willingly, believing we need to hide from God—the only One who can save us from death. In this tragic encounter we can see clearly the nature of sin and Satan—the great liar—and ourselves, who would rather listen to the lies of death than the words of life.

THOUGHTS BEFORE GOD:

God, help me not to hide from You. Give me the courage to show You who and what I am—with all my failings and brokenness. I know that You know these things already; yet somehow I still seek to hide from You. I want to stop hiding and start walking freely with You again.

☙ CREATION AND FALL—*Gen. 3:14-24*

Cursed is the ground because of you; through painful toil
you will eat of it all the days of your life (Gen. 3:17).

Part of the consequence of the Fall is that we now live in a fallen world. We can hardly imagine what it was like before sin entered. Martin Luther describes a world in which man and woman and the animals lived in peace. Lions, bears, and wolves were tame as pets. Luther suggests that even the sun shone brighter. In any case, what is certain is that the world that was our gracious and friendly host has become our enemy. Humanity must live by struggle, and so must nature. Every bird that dies from DDT poisoning dies from the results of sin. The great buffalo that were slaughtered for sport were victims of sin. Paul describes the state of nature quite clearly when he says "The whole creation has been groaning as in the pains of childbirth" (Rom. 8:22).

Sin brings death, and all creation shares the sentence of sin. Sickness and disease come from the sins of humanity and then spread their death and suffering until we forget their source. The epidemic of AIDS (acquired immunodeficiency syndrome) is only a recent example in a long history of the sin of man and woman. Genesis portrays for us in graphic terms what the results of sin are. Like a terrible cancer, it permeates the paradise that once was (or could have been) ours. Yet somehow sin succeeds in being portrayed as the "good life." It is an evil magic that causes the angel of death to appear lovely, offering the pleasures of life.

☙ THOUGHTS BEFORE GOD:

Oh, how far we have fallen! How it must hurt You to see what we, through sin, have done to ourselves and our world! How blind and foolish we are to look at the wreck of sin and think it beautiful and appealing! Give us sight to see what is real.

❧ CREATION AND FALL—*Gen. 4:1-12*

And while they were in the field,
Cain attacked his brother Abel and killed him (Gen. 4:8).

Genesis makes abundantly clear that the fall into sin is rapid and deep. We can still almost smell the freshness of the Garden of Eden, and we are already faced with murder—not only murder but the murder of a *brother.* Because of the Fall we live not only in a creation groaning under the burden of sin but also in a society torn by the effects of sin. Wherever sin goes, death follows.

We don't need to look far to see this truth graphically portrayed. In Northern Ireland, Lebanon, Iraq, Iran, and Cambodia, sin breeds hatred and death. In our own country we daily read the tragic tales of robbery, murder, rape, and child abuse. One of the great questions we face is Why does God allow this to happen?

Here in Genesis lies the source of this tragedy. God willed for man and woman to live in paradise. He offered peace and fellowship with a loving God. But God let them choose for themselves. That meant allowing the possibility of the wrong choice with its consequences. Humanity chose the wrong master and brought suffering, isolation, brokenness, and death. It is, again, the great lie of sin that points our minds toward God and says, "He's to blame."

God could end it all by taking away our freedom and making us robots, or He could destroy all of sinful humanity. But love stays His hand in the hope that love can somehow redeem us to be willing children of God. *Humanity* is responsible for the destruction brought by sin. God only waits in love for us to recognize it.

❧ THOUGHTS BEFORE GOD:

Father, how You must love us! You have given us freedom and life—even at such great cost to yourself. It is a mystery for us that even the brokenness of our world is a witness to Your love. But help us understand that in all things Your love is somehow at work.

2

ABRAHAM: FAITH AND PROMISE

INTRODUCTION

In the story of Abraham we see the beginnings of our relationship with God. God shows us what He is like and what He desires from us. Abraham models the individual's proper response (with some exceptions) and what the life of obedient faith can be. The story of Abraham, like the story of creation, is full of meaning as current as this morning's paper.

QUESTIONS TO THINK ABOUT

What is the response of faith?

How is faith acting in the assurance of "things not seen"?

What happens when we "help God out"?

What is the great gift God gives to us?

What does God show us about himself?

What is the lesson to learn from the story of Abraham?

What does this speak to me in my life?

↵ ABRAHAM: FAITH AND PROMISE—*Gen. 12:1-7*

> *The LORD had said to Abram, "Leave your country,*
> *your people and your father's household and*
> *go to the land I will show you" (Gen. 12:1).*

Abraham (at this point still "Abram") is the father of the promise. He is the father of the people of Israel, the means of blessing to the whole world, indeed, to all of creation. His children truly became a great nation. How did he come to be such a remarkable figure in the history of God's dealing with men and women?

A key part of the answer to that question, though by no means the complete answer, is described in the passage of scripture listed above. God called, and Abram answered and obeyed. It wasn't that the call was easy. God called him to leave his home and relatives behind. And where was he called to go? God said, "to the land I will show you." No guarantee. No contract. Abram committed the foolish "mistake" of buying sight unseen. A "mistake," that is, except that the "contract" was with the Lord. When it is God with whom we are dealing, the normal rules no longer apply. Though every other indication says no, and our projections, plans, charts, inside information, and "sure bets," all come down against the leading of God, His is always the right way. That's a big part of what Genesis is trying to teach us.

Look at the contrast between Adam and Abram. Adam was ruler of the world with all creation at his beck and call. But he couldn't pass up an opportunity that would make him God. Where does he end up? Cast out of the garden and subject to death. Paul says Adam brought death to all of us.

Abram was a nobody from nowhere, but he obeyed the seemingly foolish call of God. Giving up his nothingness (or at least it seems like nothing from our perspective), Abraham becomes the father of nations and of the promise. Now which one was truly foolish?

↵ THOUGHTS BEFORE GOD:

Father, help me listen. In the midst of a world full of voices calling out to me, help me be tuned to hear Your voice. And help me obey—in faith. For Your call is the call of life for me.

ABRAHAM: FAITH AND PROMISE—*Gen. 13:8-17*

Go, walk through the length and breadth of the land,
for I am giving it to you (Gen. 13:17).

S ometimes we need to claim our "Promised Land" when it may not look very promising. I wonder if Abraham had any thoughts like those I would have had when Lot walked off with the best land. Here the Lord makes a point of renewing His promise to Abram while Abram is "stuck" with second-rate real estate. "Lord, if You're going to bless me, why couldn't it be with the really good real estate instead of this?" But if Abram had those kinds of feelings, he didn't express them—he just obeyed. And sure enough, that "garden" that Lot chose, with the prosperous cities of Sodom and Gomorrah nestled in there (vv. 10-11), is now a vast expanse of desert and wasteland.

It reminds me of a funny country-and-western song I heard once. The story of the lyrics went something like this: There was a well-to-do older rancher who fell in love with a pretty young woman. To keep her attention, he showered her with gifts, which succeeded until he ran out of money and all he had left was 16 acres of land somewhere in Texas. Discovering he was penniless, the young woman laughed at him and left him for someone with more money. Later we learn that the 16 acres are in downtown Houston.

There are some real similarities to this in our relationship to God and our obedience of faith. Lot leaves for the rich life, while Abram humbly accepts God's "16 acres." Lot trusts his own judgment and the wisdom of worldly measures. Abram obeys in faith and relies upon the competence and care of God. Lot finds a wasteland. Abram receives the promise.

☙ THOUGHTS BEFORE GOD:

Lord, help me trust You even when things don't seem to be going as they should. When the other person gets the promotion, the attention, or the credit, help me cling to my faith in You. You are my answer—now and forever.

✦ ABRAHAM: FAITH AND PROMISE—*Gen. 16:1-16*

The LORD has kept me from having children (Gen. 16:2).

To obtain the promise by faith often requires waiting for the Lord to move in His own time. Unfortunately, Abraham and Sarai (later "Sarah") might have thought they knew better than God, that He had forgotten, or that He couldn't be depended upon to fulfill His promise to Abraham. They had good reason. They were still waiting for the birth of a son, and Sarai was over 75 years old. She was too old to have children and "helped out" the Lord by providing a proxy to Abram by which they could have a child. It worked; that is, they did have a child—but it wasn't the child God had in mind.

There are at least three lessons to be learned from this story: (1) God will work in His own way and in His own time, whether or not it makes sense to us or fits our understanding. (2) When we try to "help" God or take over for Him, we can be sure that His plan will not work out smoothly. We humans are notoriously poor at playing God. (3) When we try to take over for God, there are often unpleasant consequences with which we'll have to live—despite the fact that He forgives us. The nation of Israel is still struggling with the descendants of Ishmael today.

I once pastored two young college students who had been caught living together secretly. They both were repentant and prayed together with me and covenanted to put their lives in order, which they did. But a few months later I needed to counsel them again about the impending birth of an unwanted child. Their sin was forgiven, but all three people will continue to pay for this couple's enterprise in lordship. Any way but God's way is always the way to trouble.

✦ THOUGHTS BEFORE GOD:

Father, help me be patient in waiting upon You. Protect me from myself and my bumbling attempts to "help You out." Teach me to wait by trusting You.

ABRAHAM: FAITH AND PROMISE—*Gen. 17:1-16*

I will confirm my covenant between me and you
and will greatly increase your numbers (Gen. 17:2).

Despite Abraham and Sarah's foolishness about Hagar and Ishmael, God still stands ready to bless. He offers an eternal covenant of blessing. He shows us a God who waits from eternity to bless us. Even though we have failed, He waits to shower His blessings upon us. We don't need to beg and plead and placate God. He is like a father at Christmas who can hardly wait to give all the gifts he has for his child. He waits anxiously for the opportunity. Our God is first a God of blessing, not of judgment.

Usually we look at the material part of the blessing. God promises to make Abraham the father of a multitude. But this is really just a result of the greatest gift of the covenant. God gives us himself. Come, He says—I will be God to you. I will give your children the land of Canaan, and I will be their God.

There will come a time (see Exod. 33) when God becomes so frustrated with His people that He offers them Canaan but wants to cease to be their God. Moses replies that it would be better to die in the wilderness than to have Canaan without God. For from this time forward the people of Israel are the people of God.

Who are we? We are the people to whom God has given himself. This is the heart of the promise, if we will covenant to belong to Him as He has offered himself to us. We say, "This God is my God, and I am His." What greater honor could we have than this? What more distinguished heritage? What more certain ground upon which to live? In the end, what does it matter what kind of church building or program we have? If we are not His, we are nothing. But if we are His—and He is ours—what more is there?

THOUGHTS BEFORE GOD:

Oh, what a gift You have given! Your gift is giving yourself to me. You have made me Yours and given yourself to me as my God. What a gracious and giving God You are! Your gifts are abundant. Your promises are overflowing. You give and give and wait to give still more. How wonderful to be Yours!

ABRAHAM: FAITH AND PROMISE—*Gen. 22:1-14*

"Here I am," he replied (Gen. 22:1, 11).

This is certainly one of the most curious episodes in the Bible. The gracious God of creation and promise calls on Abraham to kill his own son. I don't propose to explain it all in a few sentences, but I think three lessons are drawn from the story.

First, the call of God is an absolute call. There can be no partial commitment, no halfhearted service. God calls us to a completely committed relationship with Him. Such a relationship requires all that we are and all that we have. Nothing less will do.

Second, we see that the proper answer on our part must always be "Lord, here I am." Abraham was a model in his attentive listening and willing response to the call of God. When the Lord called, he was ready. Even when the demand entailed great cost, he was willing. Abraham had learned that no matter how unpromising the prospect, God's way is always the best way.

Third, God shows us something about himself. I think He was not merely testing Abraham but also sharing something special with him. Oh, the agony that journey must have held for Abraham! Every step was one step closer to the sacrifice of his son. How painful it must have been to look into Isaac's innocent eyes when he asked, "Where is the lamb?" (v. 7). His heart must have nearly burst as he took the knife to slay his son. But God didn't want the son. The place is named "The LORD Will Provide" and of this place Scripture tells us, "On the mountain of the Lord it will be provided" or "He shall be seen" (v. 14).* Tradition says that the mount was located near the site of Jerusalem—a place called Golgotha. God didn't test Abraham to show His cruelty, but His love. "Go, Abraham," He says. "Take your son and go in peace. I will pay the price for you."

✚ THOUGHTS BEFORE GOD:

Oh, the price to be paid for the blessings You have given and continue to give in abundance! My heart is filled with compassion for Abraham as he makes his journey. But he was able to take his son back home, unharmed. Instead, You made the journey with him and left Your Son in his son's place. How can I ever understand such love as this?

---

*Interpreter's Bible, ed. George Arthur Buttrick (Nashville: Abingdon Press, 1952), 1:644.

ABRAHAM: FAITH AND PROMISE—*Rom. 4:1-3, 18-25*

*Against all hope, Abraham in hope believed and
so became the father of many nations (Rom. 4:18).*

braham was a great man. What does that have to do with us? Abraham's greatness is a model for us. His greatness was in this—he believed and obeyed. When the Lord called him to go into the unknown, he believed and obeyed. When the Lord seemed to be giving him second best, he believed and obeyed. When the Lord appeared to demand the promise back, he believed and obeyed. That's why he is a great father. We don't know if he was smarter or more competent than his contemporaries. That didn't seem to be important. What was important was faithful obedience.

So what does God desire from us? Faithful obedience. He doesn't ask us all to be great evangelists or pastors. He doesn't even expect all of us to be Sunday School teachers or church board members. But we are all called to faithful obedience. That means to hold on when things are rough. That means to believe when the "evidence" says no. The lesson of Abraham shows us the results of faithful, trusting obedience. It also shows us what happens when we try to get ahead of God.

God gave Abraham a great blessing and promise. He also waits to bless us. If we will only listen and obey Him in faith, the blessings of God wait to be poured out on us. Like an anxious father, He waits to bless us. Do you believe that? Do you live as though you believe that? Abraham did. We can.

THOUGHTS BEFORE GOD:

Father, help me to be faithful and obedient as Abraham was. I don't know why I seem to have so little confidence in You sometimes or why I resist obeying You when I know it is for the best. Help me learn to simply trust and obey.

3

MOSES AND THE GOD WHO ACTS

INTRODUCTION

This week we see God as He continues to reveal himself to us through Scripture. God shows himself to us so that we might truly know Him. In time, this knowledge becomes the basis of our faith and trust in Him. Because He is who He is and acts as He acts, we can hold fast in the midst of trouble and trials.

QUESTIONS TO THINK ABOUT

What can reassure me in the midst of tribulation?
What is God's attitude toward my situation?
How can I know what kind of deity our God is?
Why do we become impatient and upset with God?
What is the most important part of who and what I am?

⌖ MOSES AND THE GOD WHO ACTS—*Exod. 2:11-25*

So God looked on the Israelites and
was concerned about them (Exod. 2:25).

The people of Israel had gone down to Egypt with great hopes. Joseph offered protection and help in a time of trouble. Because of his position and influence, they were received as honored guests, but time passed, and what had looked so promising became enslaving. The people had forgotten who they were and where they belonged. They had become content to be "Egyptians" and had forgotten they were God's people.

The Pharaohs, too, had forgotten who the people of Israel were. The former Pharaohs had died, and those who now ruled didn't know Joseph. The people of Israel were no longer honored guests but foreign, and potentially dangerous, servants. So in the course of time the people of Israel became oppressed slaves.

Moses appears in the story (at the beginning of Exodus) as the miraculous hope for the people. But hopes are dashed as he is driven into exile and seems lost forever to the people. In their agony, the people cry out in a groaning of suffering and hopelessness. God hears them—and remembers them.

Two lessons come clearly to light in this short narrative. First, God's guidance in love and providence for yesterday can become our bondage for today. Our hope in life is in God's fresh and living word to us as we walk in relationship together. Anything less than His ongoing leadership is a recipe for trouble.

Second, no matter how deeply in trouble we are, even if the trouble is of our own making, God is listening to our heart's cry. Today's scripture reading notes that the people of Israel merely cried out. They didn't even cry out specifically to God. But God listens from eternity for the cries of those in need and distress. He waits for us to realize our need of Him. When we call, He hears and answers.

⌖ THOUGHTS BEFORE GOD:

Lord, help me keep tuned to Your voice. And help me remember that You are tuned to mine. Help me really know that You are listening, even when I'm feeling lost and alone.

MOSES AND THE GOD WHO ACTS—*Exod. 3:1-10*

I am sending you to Pharaoh
to bring my people the Israelites out of Egypt (Exod. 3:10).

In today's reading God is revealing the kind of God He is and what His intentions are for us. He responds to the cries of need and hurt by seeking relief for the Israelites. God is a God who responds in love and concern. He desires liberation for us from the oppression of slavery. It is His intention to bring us out of Egypt (slavery) into "a land flowing with milk and honey" (v. 8).

God desires the best for us. When He calls us, He calls us for our good. The idea of God wanting to make us do what we least want is false. If He calls us to where we don't want to go, it is because He knows what is best for us. Often we find that what we sought most fiercely to avoid is what we would have desired most had we understood it. God does not make us miserable. However, we make ourselves miserable when we avoid His will for us.

God is showing us a basic truth about himself. He reveals himself as the God who responds to hurt with a desire to heal. He reveals himself as the God who desires to bring the slave to freedom. He seeks to transport the sufferer to a place of healing prosperity. God is benevolent toward us—loving in all His works. The picture of an angry, vengeful God, a God of judgment, is a picture out of context. The true perspective shows a God who, from the beginning of time and through time, responds in love and concern to the hurt and suffering of His children. He loves us and desires the best for us. This picture of God transcends all others.

THOUGHTS BEFORE GOD:

Father, thank You for being concerned about my life. Thank You for caring about the little things as well as the big things. Help me remember that You're there waiting—in love.

❧ MOSES AND THE GOD WHO ACTS—*Exod. 3:13-20*

What is his name? (Exod. 3:13).

Today's scripture text is an important one to understand, for God tells Moses—and us—His own name, thereby describing *who He is*. His answer to Moses' question comes in verse 14 and is really untranslatable. It is a repetition of the verb meaning "to be." What He is saying is that He, God, *is* (that is, can be understood or defined by) what He *does*. He can be known by His acts in history. Who is God? God is the One who created in gracious providence. He is the One who was faithful to Abraham. He is the One who had a listening ear for those in distress. He is the One who sought liberation for His enslaved people.

God isn't really defined (though we sometimes think so) by omniscience, omnipotence, and omnipresence. He defines himself by His actions (toward us). History is a chalkboard upon which God uses sweeping strokes to write who He is—not only who He was and is now but also who He will continue to be. God is a God who acts redemptively and in love. That's the way He has always acted and will always act.

A large part of worship is remembering God's activity in the history of the Church and of our own personal lives. I am reminded of His love and faithfulness to Abraham, Isaac, Jacob, David, Peter, Paul, and to me. Because of this reminder of God's gracious self-revelation in the past (including *my* past), I draw encouragement for today and hope for tomorrow. My God shows me who He is in His loving, redeeming, reconciling activity—yesterday, today, and forever.

❧ THOUGHTS BEFORE GOD:

God, thank You for acting in the world and in my life. I think of my history with You and am reminded of Your faithfulness and Your love and Your care. I know that as You have been faithful in my past, You will be faithful today and tomorrow.

MOSES AND THE GOD WHO ACTS—*Exod. 5:10-23*

Why didst thou ever send me? (Exod. 5:22, RSV).

How easy it is to look back on the people of Israel and see how shortsighted and foolish they were! Here they are complaining, when in just the course of a few more chapters, God is going to miraculously deliver them. Of course, the problem is they couldn't peek into the next chapters any more than *we* can look into our future. The fact is—we are much like those foolish Israelites.

It seems to be a principle of the Christian life that our times of greatest victory are often immediately preceded by a period of trouble. In a sense, these seasons of trouble often prepare the way for the victory. They aren't just accidents that happen prior to times of victory. "Exodus" costs something. There is truly a sense (the absolute sense) in which God's grace comes to us without cost. But there is also a sense in which it demands the absolute cost from us—daily. God's grace and blessings break in freely, but they tend to break in where a person or people have given all to, and for, Him. It's not that we earn those blessings—we could never do that. Perhaps our submission somehow allows God to bless us. I can't say for sure. What does seem sure is that "exodus," spiritual victory, often comes during or after distress.

What is the key to reaching "exodus" through distress? It is faith in God's promises and faithfulness to us. "For I know whom I have believed, and am persuaded that he is able to keep that which I have committed unto him against that day" (2 Tim. 1:12, KJV).

Hold on, child of God. Keep the faith for a few more chapters. The King of Kings is on His throne, and He's in control. The "exodus" is coming.

THOUGHTS BEFORE GOD:

Father, help me have faith and trust You even in times of trouble. Help me remember that the future belongs to You and to hold on to Your promises of who You are and what You will do. Help me know that You are in control—right now.

✦ Moses and the God Who Acts—*Exod. 14:10-30*

Why are you crying out to me?
Tell the Israelites to move on (Exod. 14:15).

Those foolish Israelites! How quickly they forget God's faithfulness and care. They are barely out of Egypt, and they complain at the first sign of trouble. They have already forgotten God's mighty acts of power performed to free them. Oh, those foolish Israelites—how like us they are!

It seems to be another principle of the Christian life that we often face special trouble *following* a special victory. The great victory at the altar on Sunday is followed by a crisis at work on Monday. The Lord solves a financial problem for us, and we immediately encounter another one. Like the Israelites, we often turn to God and complain. Or we despair. We forget that God, who has been faithful and sufficient in the past, will continue to take care of us.

It is not that our problems aren't real. It was a real army chasing Moses and his people. If they could catch the Israelites, the result would be a one-sided slaughter. The Israelites weren't fussing about imaginary dangers—death was coming over the horizon at a full gallop. Christianity doesn't mean our problems disappear or turn out to be illusions. Christianity is faith in a God who is greater than any problem, as real and as threatening as they come. He can handle it. And He *will* handle it.

Remember that God has shown us who He is—the God who acts and can be known by His historic acts. The God who called Abraham, provided Isaac, and led Moses to free the people is still the same today. His intention is clear—He loves us. His power has been demonstrated again and again.

✦ Thoughts Before God:

Help me trust You, Lord. How quickly I forget! You have been so faithful to me. Help me remain patiently faithful to You.

❧ Moses and the God Who Acts
—Exod. 33:1-3, 12-16; 34:9

If your Presence does not go with us,
do not send us up from here (Exod. 33:15).

The children of Israel had been faithless again. Impatient, untrusting, they created a god in a golden calf rather than trust in the God who had demonstrated His faithfulness. Finally God tells Moses to take the people and that He would give them the land He had promised—but He would no longer go with them. Here is Moses' reply: "Lord, if you will not go with us, then let us die here. Without you, we are nothing" (author's paraphrase).

Moses knew what made the people of Israel special. It wasn't their skills or wealth or beauty or spiritual sensitivity. It was in the fact that Yahweh had made them His people and was their God. Without Him, they were just another band of wandering nomads.

Without God, we are nothing. It doesn't matter if our choir is the best in town, our sanctuary the most beautiful, our preaching the most polished, and our programs the most successful. Without God, our churches are just clubs doing little of consequence. We have no other importance—no other claim to significance. If God's living presence isn't the center of who we are and what we do, then we might as well close up and go home.

On the other hand, if we are His and He is ours, we have everything. If the choir sings flat, the sanctuary isn't beautiful, and the preaching isn't the best, it's all right. Oh, we want to have the best program, music, and preaching that we can, but that's all secondary. If He is there, what more can we ask? What greater honor could we have? How much more important could we be? The King of Kings and Lord of Lords is our God—and we are His children.

❧ Thoughts Before God:

Lord, help us always remember that You are our treasure. How quickly we begin to point to other things! Remind us that without You we are nothing—but that when You are present with us, we have all we desire.

4

DAVID

INTRODUCTION

David represents in a special way what it means to be human before God. David knew success and failure—but always in a very human way. We can identify with David. This makes an understanding of him important, especially when we realize that he seemed to hold a special place in God's heart—despite, or because of, his typical humanity. In David we see a larger-than-life reflection of ourselves involved in the struggle to live righteously before God.

QUESTIONS TO THINK ABOUT

What is the real key to our strength?

Why is patience often a spiritual virtue?

What brings us to sin?

What is the only wise response in sin?

What is the great lie of sin?

What is the final reassurance of the story of David?

What does the story of David say to me?

DAVID—*1 Sam. 17:37, 45-49*

For the battle is the LORD's,
and he will give all of you into our hands (1 Sam. 17:47).

David occupies a special place in the history of God's people. If God ever had a favorite, it seems to have been David. He models for us the best and worst of the Christian life. The story of his battle with Goliath is a favorite that we learn as young children. Perhaps because we learn it young, we often ignore it as we grow older. But in God's kingdom it is often the young who are wiser than the older and more experienced. In some ways David is at the peak of his success here, and it is from his success that we should try to learn.

Actually David was too young to really know how the world operated. He was immature enough to fail to understand the need for armor in combat. He had never seen combat, not in war. His skirmishes with an occasional wild animal were not enough to prepare him. And notice—he doesn't even plan to rely on his unusual fighting skills. He believes that the Lord will deliver him.

David was too young to understand the real problems of life. He went out to face Goliath, apparently not appreciating how real the giant was—a giant who caused Israel's strongest warriors to tremble. David was so naive that he thought he could go up against real-life, flesh-and-blood problems like Goliath with something as uncertain and nebulous as "the name of the LORD of hosts" (v. 45, KJV). He hadn't yet learned that one can't deal with real-life problems by calling on an invisible, nonmaterial "reality."

David was too young to appreciate how silly he looked, claiming to be God's representative. He wasn't important or educated or even grown up. He thought he could just walk out there in faith and depend on the Lord to come to his rescue and support. He believed that God would accept him as a champion in his battle and give Goliath into his hands.

Wasn't David a naive little boy? Isn't it a good thing that we know better?

THOUGHTS BEFORE GOD:

Father, forgive me for my pride, and help me to be as trusting as David. Help me to simply rely on You. Help me to know that no problem is too great for You to conquer—and that You can conquer even through me.

❧ DAVID—1 Sam. 24:1-10

And the men of David said to him,
"Here is the day" (1 Sam. 24:4, RSV).

Today's scripture reading is the story of David's big chance. Hated and feared by Saul, he has fled to the hills, where he is pursued by Saul and his army. David and his small troop hide in one of the many caves for safety. Then along comes Saul with his army, and they take a break near that very cave. Seeking some privacy, Saul chooses the very cave where David is hiding. David is so close that he is able to cut a piece of Saul's robe without Saul's even knowing.

Here is David's chance to kill Saul. His men encourage him; this is the way to become king. When will he ever have an opportunity like this again? However, David knows this is not God's time. So he passes up the "opportunity of a lifetime."

This story is in many ways the opposite of the story of Abraham, Sarah, and Hagar. David was supposed to be king, but God didn't seem to be doing a very good job of placing him on the throne. There was Saul, still in command, and here was David, hiding in a cave like a common thief. Sometimes it just seems that God isn't quite up to handling things and coming through on His promise. Like Sarah and Abraham, David has the opportunity to help things along, but unlike Sarah and Abraham, David stays his hand and leaves the results up to God.

Choosing to be content with God's plan and timing, David remains a refugee in the hills. But he is a refugee *in the process of becoming king.* Surer hands than his are bringing the situation to its intended conclusion. Better timing than his has set the timetable. David has chosen a better guarantee for his future than he could provide with a quick thrust of a blade. He is perhaps at his greatest here. It couldn't have been easy to pass up this kind of opportunity. But he did—giving up the "opportunity of a lifetime" for the promise of the God who acts in His own time. As it turned out, it wasn't a bad trade.

❧ THOUGHTS BEFORE GOD:

Father, help me be patient and obedient. Help me be content, in fullness or in want, as long as I am in Your will. Help me recognize the "shortcuts" of this world as long detours around the paths of Your grace and providence.

❧ DAVID—*2 Sam. 11:1-5*

But David remained in Jerusalem (2 Sam. 11:1).

*O*h, David, David—how could you? Reading today's passage is like watching the plot develop in a familiar old movie. You almost want to cry out to the hero, "Don't do it!" Everything worked out for David. He had everything. How far he had come from the time when he was a ragged refugee! How abundantly faithful God had been! How could David fall now?

Ironically, it is sometimes in the midst of our success that we are most apt to succumb to sin. We forget that the victory is God's, not ours. We begin to believe that we have accomplished these things, and we become self-satisfied. David put himself in trouble's way when he stayed home instead of going to war. He had become complacent. He had just won a great victory over Syria. He didn't need to bother with the cleanup action on the Ammonites. His kingdom was secure, and his armies were strong. It was time to sit back and enjoy what he had accomplished.

There are at least two lessons to learn from this sad episode in David's life. The first is that big sins follow a trail of small ones. We don't usually backslide in a moment of temptation. We may take an important step in that direction, but the way is almost always prepared by a process of drifting away from God. Our time with the Lord dwindles. Our attitude worsens. Worship becomes a burden. We enjoy the times of fellowship less, particularly when there is a spiritual emphasis. Others may not even notice. We may not even realize what we are doing. But suddenly we find ourselves looking at sin, and it has become very beautiful. We don't feel ourselves resisting. The long journey from God's grace to a broken relationship has somehow taken place almost without noticing.

Second, it doesn't matter where we are—sin leads us on a one-way journey into brokenness. David had the world by the tail when God had him by the hand. But once he chose sin, he was on the road to losing what he had. In faithful obedience, he had been a refugee in the process of becoming king. In sin he was a prosperous king in the process of becoming a refugee.

❧ THOUGHTS BEFORE GOD:

Father, keep me from forgetting that You are the Source of all I am or hope to be. Help me see what sin really offers me. Help me trust You and be patient in Your leadership and care and not complacent in my own accomplishments.

✺ David—*2 Sam. 12:1-9, 13-19*

David said to Nathan,
"I have sinned against the LORD" (2 Sam. 12:13).

You can be sure that hidden sins will come to light. Yet often people are *surprised* to find that their crimes or sins have been discovered. Somehow we believe we can hide them. But God is watching, even if no one else is. David thought he had solved his problem. Uriah was dead, and Bathsheba had become his wife—end of trouble. Unfortunately, he was living in a fool's paradise.

However, it must be added that even in this sad encounter, David displays the spiritual sensitivity that makes him special. When confronted with his sin, he doesn't hide or rationalize (as Adam and Eve did); he confesses and repents. By doing so, he reveals the real mark of a mature relationship with God.

We all have failed or will fail in our walk with God. One just cannot live on the mountaintop all the time. Somewhere along the way, no matter how hard we try, we're going to fail. The mark of the victorious Christian is not that he or she never has trouble, but that he or she is quick to repent and keep on going. Sin works in us (like Adam and Eve) to keep us from simple confession. Something in us wants to keep our shortcomings hidden even from God. But David shows, even in his terrible sin, the simple answer. When God taps us on the shoulder and points to our sin (which we thought we could hide), the correct answer is "Yes, I have sinned against the Lord."

These simple words are the hardest to say, but they are the beginning of healing and a sign that we are heading in the right direction. David's sin would bear terrible consequences. But he is on the way to redemption already.

✺ THOUGHTS BEFORE GOD:

Lord, help me know that all things are known to You. And when You remind me, help me be ready to admit my need of You. Take away my pride, and give me a spirit of repentance before You.

↝ David—*2 Sam. 12:10-12*

> *Now, therefore, the sword will never depart*
> *from your house (2 Sam. 12:10).*

Sin is offered to humanity on a great "enjoy now—pay later" plan. We almost forget the latter part. Sometimes we think it is God who wants to punish us for having a good time. How twisted our thinking becomes! Sin comes with strings attached and consequences that follow. Long after the "pleasure" is over, we, or others, will be paying the price.

In David's case, the results of this sin will follow him all his life. One son will rape his own half sister. Her full brother will kill the half brother and flee in exile. Eventually he will return to ravage the kingdom and debase David's house. David took Bathsheba in secret. Absalom will take David's concubines "in the sight of all Israel" (16:22). Even David's eventual victory is bittersweet because of the death of his son Absalom. There is no need to wonder what he would say if we could ask him if his sin was worth it. We know the answer.

Yet how often do we reenact David's tragedy? Again and again, people are surprised to encounter the cost of their sin. How many have said the words "I never realized . . ."? Sin is a terrible, terrible thing. If it is puritan or old-fashioned to say so, then so be it. But I have seen enough tears and brokenness to be angry at the lie of easy tolerance—"as long as it doesn't hurt anybody." Doesn't it? Sin is a destroyer. Brokenness, pain, and suffering follow in its wake. It is not a sign of sophistication to be soft on sin. It is a sign of foolishness or ignorance. If you asked David, he would tell you.

↝ Thoughts Before God:

Father, help us hate and fear sin. Help us love the people it is destroying. But help us see sin for what it is, despite the attractive wrapping and the promises. Save us from the lies we have believed and are still tempted to believe.

❧ DAVID—*Luke 2:1-7*

Because he belonged to the house and line of David (Luke 2:4).

To get to the end of the story of David, we really have to jump all the way to the New Testament. Here we find David as the forefather of Jesus. This really tells us something about God and His relationship to us. It also tells us something about our lives.

Despite his sin, David is still the earthly parent of Jesus (though generations removed). God doesn't throw him away and look for a new specimen. He accepts him as he is—a repentant sinner. That is also the ground of *our* acceptance into the Kingdom and our continued acceptance. David not only continues to be accepted by God but also seems to be a favorite of God's. Despite his failures and shortcomings, and in all of his humanity, God loves him with a tender love.

God isn't looking for perfect people—He's looking for repentant people. He shows us from David to Hosea to the prodigal son that He waits for us to allow Him to love us as we turn to Him. David did some foolish things. He also did some terrible and cruel things. But in his repentance God loved him. And God made David His own, even to the point of making him the forefather of Christ. He waits for us in the same way. No matter what we have done or may do, He waits only for our submission in repentance to allow His love to flow like a mighty river about us.

❧ THOUGHTS BEFORE GOD:

Lord, help me know that I cannot, and need not, earn Your love. Help me realize that You truly love and accept me in all of my humanity. Help me know the warmth of Your love.

5

Servanthood

Introduction

The Book of Isaiah portrays the work of God and anticipates the coming of Christ. The prophet reveals what Christ will do and what we should be. Servanthood is a difficult lesson to accept and learn.

Questions to Think About

What is the model of servanthood Isaiah presents for us?

What is God's attitude toward us?

What does servanthood have to do with everyday life?

What is the promise of servanthood?

What is the nature of the life of servanthood?

What is God's call upon us?

How does Isaiah give me guidance in servanthood?

How does Isaiah give me hope in servanthood?

What does Isaiah teach us about God in Christ?

❧ SERVANTHOOD—*Isa. 53:3-9*

Surely he took up our infirmities and carried our sorrows,
yet we considered him stricken by God,
smitten by him, and afflicted (Isa. 53:4).

The Book of Isaiah paints a graphic picture of what is called the Suffering Servant. It portrays the suffering nation of Judah and anticipates the coming of Christ. There are two major themes of prophetic anticipation of the Messiah. One is that of the triumphant Son of God (see 9:2-7). This is the expectation of a Messiah who will come in glory and victorious power—which He does. But the other theme tells the nature of that glory and power. In 53:3-9 we find the overcoming power and glory of the Suffering Servant of God.

What a paradox! God triumphs in suffering; He conquers by His death. He is exalted through humiliation; He reigns by humble service. No wonder the Jews weren't looking for such a Messiah!

God in Christ portrays for us His kingdom, which is not like the kingdoms of this world. In doing so, He not only shows His own nature and the extent of His love but also models a life of servanthood for us. The life of ministry is a life of fullness and meaning and overcoming. But it is often all these things precisely in terms of suffering service. Others may be healed by our stripes. We carry the wounds in our bodies and minds to facilitate the healing of others. We have no promise of reward or earthly success or recognition. We give and serve that others might be healed. It is, in many ways, a daily dying in servanthood.

If it sounds difficult and sometimes painful, that's because it is. But Christ is our model. He has led the way before us with His broken body and shed blood. It is when we share that suffering service that we are most like Him.

❧ THOUGHTS BEFORE GOD:

Lord, we would so much rather be served than serve, be free of suffering than suffer. Give us the courage and commitment and faith to take up our crosses and follow You.

✣ Servanthood—*Isa. 55:1-7*

Come, all you who are thirsty, come to the waters (Isa. 55:1).

I f there is one thing I have learned about God, it is this: He stands from eternity to eternity with open arms of love toward us. It took me a long time to learn this, and I still have trouble believing it.

The concept of the Righteous Judge is easy—I learned about Him early and well. I remember staying home from church one Sunday night as a young boy. It was a stormy evening, and with every clash of thunder I hoped the Lord would not return. If He came and I was not at church, I feared I would be damned to hell.

It's not that we want to escape the righteous demands of God. It's not that faithful participation in community is not important, but our understanding of God's attitude toward us needs to be redeemed. Rather than the Triumphant King coming on wings of glory to judge and destroy, Jesus comes as the Suffering Servant with outstretched arms of love. He does not accept us in our sin. In love He calls us out of our sin.

When the final Judgment does come and those who choose are lost forever, I don't believe that God will display a mood of triumph. Even as He sends them away, I see tears streaming down His face. If they have insisted upon "freedom" from God, then He must finally let them go. But it was for these He came and suffered. It is for these that His love is poured out. It is for these—for us—that He waits with open arms of love.

> *See, on the portals He's waiting and watching,*
>
> . . . .
>
> *Calling, "O sinner, come home!"*
>
> —Will L. Thompson

✣ Thoughts Before God:

Forgive us, Father, for our harsh picture of You. Help us understand that You call us to righteousness as a way to life. Help us see You and emulate You in Your open call of forgiving love.

✦ SERVANTHOOD—*Isa. 58:6-12*

> *Is not this the kind of fasting I have chosen:*
> *to loose the chains of injustice?* (Isa. 58:6).

The Jews were always a religious people. They practiced the feasts and ceremonies of Yahweh—even while worshiping other gods. They attended church, gave their tithes, sang in the choir, and served on the board. But God said it wasn't enough. Just as He revealed himself by His participation in history, so we are called to live out our faith. We are not merely to be *called* Christians but to *be* Christians.

Poor religion does not address the way in which one conducts his or her business. Empty religion does not address home and family. If one's religion does not go beyond church services, then it is not really engaged with life. Our lives are primarily lived at home, at work—with friends, enemies, and family.

God is saying to the people of Judah that He's not in the fasting-feasting business. He's in the wicked-bondage-breaking business. Our faith should address the totality of our lives. Out of the context of my values and goals, I should determine what to buy, where to live, and how to live. Servanthood is not a Sunday or "someday" kind of lifestyle. It colors and shapes our whole lives. God wants to change not only our churches but also our lives, our homes, our cities, and our world. Being a servant means being a part of that plan.

✦ THOUGHTS BEFORE GOD:

Father, help us worship You with all our lives. May every part be touched and shaped by You. We want our lives to be completely Yours for Your purpose and glory.

SERVANTHOOD—*Isa. 60:1-3*

But the LORD rises upon you
and his glory appears over you (Isa. 60:2).

One part of suffering servanthood we must never forget is a triumphant life. In the suffering sacrifice of Christ, God's power was made manifest and effective. It is in the death of the humiliated Christ that God overcame Satan and death.

So it is for us. As the wounds and scars of servanthood become part of us, the glory of the Lord comes upon us. In our suffering servanthood, He suffers. And as we serve, He is lifted up. This is how in the midst of a world of darkness light breaks forth.

Look how the images are reversed: The world, triumphant and powerful, seems to overcome the apparently inferior servant. In the world, victory is light, and defeat and suffering are darkness. But this is all illusion. Through God's eyes we see the world dying—not victorious. It is covered with darkness, not light. Light comes from and by the glory of the Lord, the glory of the Suffering Servant of God. It is the victory of the One who died on the Cross.

Because Christ gave himself in suffering love for us, "every knee shall bow . . . every tongue . . . confess that Jesus Christ is Lord" (Phil. 2:10, TLB). Our wounds and scars are not signs of defeat or failure, but of success. It is a success the world does not recognize or understand. But it is a success that will finally triumph. Before the Suffering Servant, the Lamb of God, all creation will bow in final and absolute surrender.

THOUGHTS BEFORE GOD:

Lord, help us always remember that You are the Triumphant One. The victory of this world is a passing illusion. The reality of all things rests in Your hands. As we are buffeted, especially in service, help us remember that You are Lord.

↬ SERVANTHOOD—*Isa. 61:1-4*

> *The Spirit of the Sovereign LORD is on me,*
> *because the LORD has anointed me*
> *to preach good news to the poor* (Isa. 61:1).

Jesus refers specifically to today's scripture passage as marking His ministry (see Matt. 11:5 and Luke 4:18-19). His ministry was to be identified according to the standards set by this passage. It harkens to the "year of jubilee" (see Lev. 25), an old practice calling for the cancellation of debts and freedom for the imprisoned. It was a time of new life and new hope, of restoration of what was lost. Jesus proclaimed His ministry as one of hope, healing, and restoration. By identifying with the hopeless, He brought hope.

Suffering servanthood was the price to be paid for this hope. There is a price for healing. Christ paid it for us, and we, by our servanthood, help to pay it for others. Like a bridge over troubled waters, we are laid down and given to purchase the hope of jubilee.

That also means that the nature of the Christian life is hope. Christ came to bring hope, freedom, and reconciliation. That's what the Church is about. Through servanthood and submission to God, we participate in new life. The victorious Christ does not come in victory to rule over a battlefield covered with death. He comes as a Lamb to rule over fields of joy and hope. In Christ the dawn of new life begins for us and through us.

↬ THOUGHTS BEFORE GOD:

What a wonderful gospel You bring to us! Out of our brokenness You bring healing. Help us to be a people of hope in the light of Your promises to us.

⤳ SERVANTHOOD—*Isa. 66:1-2*

This is what the LORD says:
"Heaven is my throne" (Isa. 66:1).

We should never forget that the Suffering Servant, who as a meek Lamb went to slaughter, is also the King of Kings. Heaven is His throne, earth His footstool. We should neither presume nor take His presence lightly. He is truly God, and all that is He has made. When we speak of God's identification with us, we must not redefine God as more human and less divine. We cannot draw near to Him by pulling Him down. He is God forever.

The great mystery and wonder is that this God, who remains God, comes to us. He looks to us and seeks not greatness or brilliance or beauty (as the old Roman and Greek gods would), but "he who is humble and contrite in spirit, and trembles at my word" (v. 2). He seeks from us what we can offer. To come to Him we must lower ourselves— not reach up, but bow down; not in mastery of others, but in servanthood and humility. It is not our greatness that will please Him, but our lowliness.

He demands little from us. It is a simple thing to be humble before the Lord of Lords. As we serve others, we serve Him and gain His approval. It is strange that we are so reluctant to serve, curious that we resent and resist humility. Yet the King of all kings lowered himself for us. All He asks is that we do the same for Him.

⤳ THOUGHTS BEFORE GOD:

You are so great that it is beyond our imagination to know You. Yet You come to us and humble yourself for us. How little You ask when You call us to serve! Help us serve You with joy.

6

THE LOVE OF GOD

INTRODUCTION

Hosea is one of the most powerful books in the Old Testament. In it we encounter God's love as it touches humanity's freedom. We learn the limits of God's love and the extent of our freedom as we observe His dealings with the people of Israel. As we discover "tough love" that pays a high price for the beloved, we observe the love of God that is willing to pay a high price for us.

QUESTIONS TO THINK ABOUT

What is the nature and end of sin?
What is God's attitude toward us as sinners?
What is the promise of sin?
What does sin produce out of that promise?
How enduring is God's love for us?
How dangerous is sin?
What is the image of God that is left from Hosea?

❧ The Love of God—*Hos. 1:1-9*

*Call his name Not my people, for you are not my people
and I am not your God* (Hos. 1:9, RSV).

Hosea is the last prophet to the Northern Kingdom of Israel. They have drifted away from God into a worldly sophistication. They still observe the Jewish feasts and religious observances, but they also observe those of the other religions of the area. They have become "open-minded" in their religious faith and practice an "open marriage" in their relationship with God. To graphically illustrate this infidelity in a prophetic message to the people, God calls Hosea to live out in his own life the tragedy of God's relationship with them.

In naming the children of Hosea's marriage to the unfaithful Gomer, God proclaims the broken relationship. The first child is named "Jezreel," or "God sows," pointing to the destructive consequences of sin. It is really the *people* who sow seeds of sin and await the harvest. The second child is named "not loved," for the progressive destruction of sin destroys the relationship of affection and love. The third is named "not my people," in a pronouncement of the final and ultimate break in the relationship. God finally lets them go. They walk blindly to destruction and will not hear.

C. S. Lewis writes in *The Great Divorce* that in the end two kinds of people will remain: those who allow God to have His way with them and those He finally allows to have *their own* way. Judgment is not God's imposing of His destructive will on us, but the imposition of our own destructive will upon ourselves.

❧ Thoughts Before God:

Forgive us, Lord, for portraying You as a grim, angry judge. We are the ones responsible for our brokenness and judgment. Help us see Your loving concern even in Your judgment of us.

❧ The Love of God—*Hos. 1:10-11*

In the place where it was said to them,
"You are not my people,"
they will be called "sons of the living God" (Hos. 1:10).

Verse 9 of Hosea 1 contains the ultimate judgment—the withdrawal of God's presence. It is the final concession to the expressed will of the kingdom of Israel. Yet the final judgment is immediately followed by the renewed promise of blessing and restoration. The fact that we find it here is an important indication of the nature of God's love for us.

Israel has rejected God's love, and God has let them go free, even though freedom means destruction for them. Despite their ultimate rejection of Him, God reaffirms to them His offer of reconciliation and restoration. His love transcends their rejection and His humiliation. Hosea acts out the role of the abandoned husband who waits with the offer of reconciliation and forgiveness.

God will let us condemn ourselves if we insist. But He will continue to wait from eternity to eternity with open arms of love toward us. If we will only turn to Him, we will find Him waiting to bless and restore us.

❧ Thoughts Before God:

Lord, how You must love us! When we have rejected You, scorned You, sinned against You, still You love us and desire our return to You. When we cannot love ourselves, You love us with perfect love.

☙ THE LOVE OF GOD—*Hos. 2:6-8*

> *She will chase after her lovers but not catch them;*
> *she will look for them but not find them (Hos. 2:7).*

This passage of scripture graphically describes the torment of sin and its failure to satisfy. When we seek fulfillment and pleasure outside of the will of God, we are condemning ourselves to more and more frantic seeking with less and less fulfilling enjoyment. Plato described the man who seeks for pleasure as being like a man trying to fill a sieve with sand—the faster he fills it, the faster it runs out. The fulfillment of sin is an ever-elusive goal that drives us on, taunts us, and finally leaves us empty.

Sin offers only a reflection or shadow of true joy. The appeal of sin is always a quicker, cheapened version of the real fulfillment in God's plan. Overindulgence in any vice is an attempt to gain, through quantity or multiple possession, what God intends to be enjoyed in moderation or exclusive relation. The lie of sin is in promising what it cannot deliver. True joy and happiness belong to God. Sin promises and then draws us into its empty trap.

God's anguished cry is that He is the One offering the joy and pleasure we truly seek. If we will seek it through Him and in His way, His blessing may truly be ours. Sin promises us what God alone can deliver.

☙ THOUGHTS BEFORE GOD:

Lord, forgive us for trying to take false shortcuts to the blessings You desire to give us. We cheapen ourselves and cause You sorrow by our frantic attempts to find fulfillment apart from You. Give us eyes to see and hearts to follow Your will.

↪ THE LOVE OF GOD—Hos. 3:1-3

The LORD said to me,
"Go, show your love to your wife again" (Hos. 3:1).

The translations of this verse vary, but the clear intent of the Hebrew is to call Hosea to continue to pursue his unfaithful wife out of his love for her. The tragic image of Hosea is a portrayal of God's love and actions for us. Hosea goes on loving Gomer even though she has fallen into the depths of humiliation. Having originally gone to enjoy the company and rewards of her lover, she has found herself going from one lover to another. Each spiral of sin descends lower and lower until she finally is reduced to a state of slavery, property to be bought and sold.

Hosea makes his way to the slave market, no doubt taunted and laughed at as his neighbors recognize the cuckold husband. There in the marketplace he buys back the wife who has abandoned and humiliated him. She is no longer the young wife he married. Her beauty and allure have been sold for pleasure and joy that vanished as quickly as they came. Yet to regain this broken shell of the woman he married, Hosea pays the price and takes her home. God has said, "Go on loving," and he will.

Hosea acts out God's part for us to see. Willing to pay the price for the ruin of sin, He gives himself for us. He shows no pride but humiliates himself for us. No price is too high, no cost too great.

↪ THOUGHTS BEFORE GOD:

How You love me! It is more than I can comprehend. Lord, help me live in the awareness of Your overwhelming love.

❧ THE LOVE OF GOD—*Hos. 4:17-19*

Ephraim is joined to idols; leave him alone! (Hos. 4:17).

The pronouncement of Hosea 4:17 stands as the backdrop to the awesome display of God's love seen in yesterday's text. For as great as God's love is, it cannot or will not override our free will. God's offer of love stands as an offer that may be accepted or rejected.

The final Judgment is described in today's text. Israel is bound so tightly to sin that it no longer can, or desires to, respond to God's voice. This is the "unpardonable" sin, the sin that has made us finally deaf to the call of God and blind to His loving presence. It is not that God is no longer willing to forgive—rather, we are no longer *interested* in forgiveness.

The tragedy of Hosea's ministry is that it failed in the sense that Israel chose not to respond. God called with a love that could overcome any obstacle except their rejection. But they chose their own way. They were too sophisticated to be bound to an old-fashioned relationship to a God who demanded an exclusive relationship with Him. They had outgrown God.

In approximately 721 B.C. the Northern Kingdom of Israel fell. The inhabitants were scattered. The 10 tribes who made up the Northern Kingdom were "lost." After this time, when we talk about Israel, we are really talking about the Southern Kingdom of Judah. God loved the lost tribes. He wanted to restore them—to save them. But He let them have their own way when nothing He could do or say would cause them to change their minds. They were lost forever.

❧ THOUGHTS BEFORE GOD:

O Lord, help us never take lightly the consequences and the danger of sin. Help us not to presume upon Your grace. How You must grieve for Your lost children! Help us learn from their error.

↪ THE LOVE OF GOD—Hos. 14

I will heal their waywardness and love them freely,
for my anger has turned away from them (Hos. 14:4).

Hosea ends with the offer and call to reconciliation and restoration. Despite their denial that will prove to be final, God ends with an invitation of grace. The message is emphatically clear. God desires our return to Him no matter how far we may have fallen. He loves us no matter how deep or despicable our sin. He continues to desire and pursue us no matter how persistent the patterns of sin in our lives. He longs to restore us no matter how many times we have failed Him.

Many Christians, as well as those who have tried and given up on Christianity, are defeated by their sin. They allow their past or present sin to become a barrier between themselves and God. They despair of being holy or virtuous enough to bring those laurels to place at Jesus' feet. All they have to bring is their failure or sin. So like the rich ruler, they go away sorrowfully, wistfully wishing they could have been good enough to be a Christian.

But this passage and indeed the whole story of Hosea tell us that God does not desire a barrier between us. He does not intend that our sins should separate us from Him. He desires the surrender of our sin to Him. It is the confession of our sin and our utter dependence upon Him that He desires from us.

The Book of Hosea ends with a picture of the waiting God. With promises of forgiveness, restoration, and blessing, He waits for us. He's still waiting.

↪ THOUGHTS BEFORE GOD:

Lord, help me be quick to bring my failures to You, quick to confess them, and quick to surrender them to You. Help me not let the evil one convince me that You do not want me to come or that I am not worthy enough to come. Unworthy as I am, You love me into eternity.

7

Mark:
The Kingdom Has Come

Introduction

Mark's Gospel gives us a living account of the life of Jesus. Mark draws from Peter and other witnesses to give a "you are there" quality to the story of Jesus' life and ministry. He invites us to be participating observers, permitting us also to be responsive hearers of Jesus' call to follow Him.

Questions to Think About

What is Mark trying to accomplish with his record of Jesus' life?
What kinds of claims does the Gospel of Mark make about Jesus?
What kinds of claims does it make on us?
What response do *you* give to the story of Jesus?
Who will tell the unfinished story?

✷ MARK: THE KINGDOM HAS COME—*Mark 1:14-20*

The kingdom of God is near. Repent and believe. . . .
At once they left their nets and followed (Mark 1:15, 18).

In this brief passage we receive the message of the Gospel in summary. All the rest of Mark's Gospel will be an expansion of this central message. It begins by declaring that the kingdom of God has come in the person of Jesus Christ. Centuries of anticipation and hope have now reached their fulfillment. History itself has arrived at a point of culmination. Even the end of time will only be a completion of this coming.

This truth requires a response and demands a decision. We must either leave the past behind or deny the truth by continuing unchanged. We cannot avoid or compromise; we must decide. Yes or no. The Kingdom has come in Christ, or it hasn't.

The disciples' response is intended as our model. When they heard the pronouncement that the Kingdom had come, they left their nets and their former lives behind. That is why Jesus came and why Mark tells the story. The proclamation of Mark's Gospel is intended to achieve a real, living response. Mark's Gospel is really an evangelistic presentation of the life of Jesus that extends an invitation and calls for a response.

Jesus is the realization and fulfillment of all you are hoping and longing for. He is here for *you*. He invites you to be His disciple and leave the past behind. Will you believe? Will you follow?

✷ THOUGHTS BEFORE GOD:

Jesus, You are all I have been looking for. You are the answer to my life's needs. For Your sake I will abandon all to follow You and be Your disciple.

❧ MARK: THE KINGDOM HAS COME—*Mark 4:35-41*

They were terrified and asked each other, "Who is this?
Even the wind and the waves obey him!" (Mark 4:41).

Mark gives us a front-row seat at one of the most dramatic and exciting events in Jesus' ministry. What a scene! A violent storm, characteristic of the Sea of Galilee, breaks suddenly around the disciples' boat. You can almost hear the wind shrieking and feel the boat reeling. The men are drenched by the cold waves that crash over the sides of the small boat. Cries of desperation are heard above the sounds of the storm as seasoned sailors struggle to save the ship. The disciples, who were not sailors by trade, huddle in panicked fear. Minutes seem like hours as they endure the torment.

Then there is Jesus. The disciples are struck by His casual behavior. The contrast to their desperation and fear was striking. Head on a pillow, a look of peaceful contentment on His sleeping face, Jesus is the picture of calm and serene confidence. Once awakened by their loud complaints, He rebukes the wind and calls the waves to be still. Suddenly everything around them is as peaceful and serene as Jesus himself.

There are at least two messages here. One is that Mark intends that we should see ourselves in the disciples. They act as we would act, respond as we would respond. And we should be amazed, as they were amazed. Surely this Man Jesus transcends the boundaries of our experience and understanding. He confounds the categories. He calls our world into question by His presence and power.

The second is a message for disciples. When we find ourselves overtaken by the sudden and sometimes devastating storms of life, we are often like Jesus' disciples. Frantic and desperate, we struggle to regain control. Frightened, we panic, and the storm defeats us. Frustrated, we accuse God of indifference. Through it all, Jesus is there sharing our lives and our distress, yet in serene confidence.

"Don't You care?" we cry.

With patient love He replies, "Won't you trust Me?"

❧ THOUGHTS BEFORE GOD:

Jesus, thank You for walking among us and revealing yourself. Forgive me for being so slow to recognize You. Forgive me for being so quick to doubt You. When my boat is tossed in the storm, help me trust You.

❧ MARK: THE KINGDOM HAS COME—*Mark 8:27-38*

"Who do you say I am?"
Peter answered, "You are the Christ." . . .
"If anyone would come after me, he must deny himself
and take up his cross and follow me" (Mark 8:29, 34).

At the encounter in today's scripture reading between Jesus and the disciples, we touch the heart of Mark's Gospel. Before this point we read account after account of the miracles and demonstrations of power and authority that accompany Christ's ministry. These events are punctuated by the crowds asking, "Who is this Man?"

Jesus asks the disciples (and the readers), "Who do *you* say I am? You have seen what I have done. You have witnessed My life. Now you must decide what you believe about Me. Am I to be believed or not?"

Faced with that question, Peter rises to the occasion. "You are the Christ" (v. 29), he declares. In this confession, Peter also expresses our response: "Yes, Lord, You are the Christ. You are the One we have been looking for."

Immediately Jesus adds the commitment that must accompany Peter's (and our) confession: "If you want to claim Me, you must follow Me. Acknowledging Me as the Christ means accepting My claim upon your life. It means taking up your cross and following Me along the path of love and service I walk before you. It means dying to your old life and your old ways and taking up My life—even to the point of physical death. When you confess My Lordship, you must also accept and live it."

Here we come to the heart of Mark's Gospel. It is also the heart of the message of Jesus Christ. "Who do you say that I am? Will you take up your cross and follow Me?"

❧ THOUGHTS BEFORE GOD:

Jesus, I confess that You are the Christ. I also confess that I want to discover You as the Christ without following You along the way of the Cross. Help me confess You as Lord with my life as well as with my worship. Help me confess You as Lord by taking up my cross and following You.

↝ MARK: THE KINGDOM HAS COME—*Mark 12:13-17*

*Then Jesus said to them, "Give to Caesar what is Caesar's
and to God what is God's"* (Mark 12:17).

This brief exchange between Jesus and some Pharisees is both delightful and earnestly challenging. These clever Pharisees planned to entrap Jesus by posing a politically compromising dilemma for Him to solve. First they praise Him for His courageous commitment to truth regardless of the consequences. Then they ask Him whether they ought to pay taxes to Caesar. That is, should they support the oppressive occupation of the land of Israel by a pagan conqueror? Should they be partners-by-participation with these enemies of the true God?

The Pharisees appear smug. Jesus is seemingly ensnared. If He says they should pay taxes (and so support the hated Romans and the corrupt tax collectors), the people will reject Him. If He says they should not, the Romans will regard Him as an open revolutionary. It appears He has nowhere to go.

However, Jesus successfully meets their challenge. He refers to a Roman coin, stamped with Caesar's image. It and the ministry of government are a product of Caesar. Give Caesar what is his. On the other hand, give God what is His and bears *His* image. What is it that bears God's image? (Gen. 1:27 answered that for us long ago: "In the image of God he created him." *Humanity* bears God's image as clearly as the Roman coin bears Caesar's image. Give Caesar appropriate civic service. God's claim on you is much deeper. All that you are belongs to Him.

Mark 12:17 says the Pharisees were amazed at Jesus, and rightfully so. He took their clever scheme and entrapped them in it. We, too, are included in Jesus' statement. What bears God's image should be surrendered to Him. Our basic humanity, our fundamental identity, the heart and soul of who and what we are needs to be surrendered to God.

↝ THOUGHTS BEFORE GOD:

Lord, forgive me for forgetting that all I am is a creative gift from You. Help me completely surrender to You, the One whose image I bear.

❧ MARK: THE KINGDOM HAS COME—*Mark 15:33-39*

And when the centurion, who stood there in front of Jesus,
heard his cry and saw how he died, he said,
"Surely this man was the Son of God!" (Mark 15:39).

Mark has given us an eyewitness view of Jesus' life and ministry. We stood with the crowd and watched the miracles Jesus performed. We sat cold, wet, and terrified in the boat with Jesus in the storm and witnessed His amazing power. We journeyed to the home of a small girl and death's bedside and heard Jesus declare His Lordship and power over that frightening enemy. We walked to the garden and watched Jesus' arrest and trial. Now we stand at the foot of the Cross with the centurion and witness Jesus' own death.

Jesus' death, like His life, is extraordinary. With incomprehensible grace, He endures the unspeakable agonies of crucifixion. Even while impaled on a cross, He exerts a special power over those around Him. His death might have been expected to come in a whimper of suffering or a curse of anger. But it doesn't. Drawing His final reserves of strength, He cries out in a loud voice. Not in despair. Not in anger. In triumph and overcoming faith, He entrusts himself to the Father, declaring, "It is finished" (John 19:30). His mission completed successfully, He crosses the finish line a victor.

Having witnessed this extraordinary end to this extraordinary life, the centurion is moved to confess Jesus as the Son of God. We, too, watching with the centurion, are moved to confess Jesus as Lord. The Kingdom has come, the invitation extended. Will we repent and believe and follow Jesus?

❧ THOUGHTS BEFORE GOD:

Lord, thank You. Thank You for the life You lived and the death You died. You deserve my worship and obedience. You compel my confession and repentance. Help me follow You truly and faithfully.

❧ MARK: THE KINGDOM HAS COME—*Mark 16:1-8*

*Trembling and bewildered, the women went out
and fled from the tomb. They said nothing to anyone,
because they were afraid (Mark 16:8).*

Throughout his Gospel, Mark has drawn us into the story of Jesus' life. He has written his account of Jesus' life so that we feel we are actually there. He has made us witnesses of this incredible story. Jesus has overwhelmed our ability to comprehend Him. He has frustrated our every attempt to reduce Him to our level of understanding.

Through Mark's account we have seen the miracles, heard the teaching, witnessed Jesus' death, and discovered His empty tomb. Jesus' remarkable story ends with the ultimate miracle.

Hopefully along the way we have moved from skeptics to disciples. We, too, believe. Jesus has become our hope, and we have committed to follow Him.

The women in this passage discovered an empty tomb. The death and suffering of Christ was swallowed up in life. The power of life overcame the power of suffering and death, and death cannot be found. Here lies the greatest victory of the gospel story.

The final victory must be told. This is the compelling commission of the first believers—and our commission as well.

❧ THOUGHTS BEFORE GOD:

Here I am, Lord. I am a witness. I must go and share the wonderful, life-changing story. Help me, Lord, to deny my fears and tell my world the story of Jesus so that they, too, can know Him.

8

PENTECOST

INTRODUCTION

Pentecost tells the story of the coming of the Holy Spirit upon the Church. The impact of that event on the disciples of Christ and on the city of Jerusalem was amazing. Common people, empowered by the presence of the Holy Spirit, literally changed the world. Part of the message of Pentecost is that the same Holy Spirit is available to us.

QUESTIONS TO THINK ABOUT

What is the importance of the Holy Spirit for the Church?
What is the purpose of the giving of the Holy Spirit to the Church?
What is the good news that the coming of the Holy Spirit brings?
What is the Holy Spirit's primary purpose?
How important is the Holy Spirit for the work of the Church?

↷ PENTECOST—*Acts 1:1-5*

*John baptized with water, but in a few days
you will be baptized with the Holy Spirit* (Acts 1:5).

For 40 days the resurrected Jesus appeared to His disciples and talked to them about the kingdom of God. Of all those conversations, Luke chooses the brief announcement in today's scripture reading as the one message to record. In fact, it serves to introduce the whole Book of Acts. This announcement, the coming of the Holy Spirit upon the disciples, had profound implications for the future work of the Kingdom in the world.

It was a *commissioning*. Jesus related the Spirit to the initiation of His own ministry. In Luke 4:18, Jesus proclaims His ministry by quoting the prophet Isaiah: "The Spirit of the Lord is on me." As the Spirit had been with Jesus, He would now be given to the disciples. The ministry that Jesus had begun would be carried out by His disciples under the power and direction of the Holy Spirit.

It would be an intimate *relationship*. In Luke 10:17-22, Jesus shares an unusually personal moment with His disciples. They are permitted to share in a time of special closeness and joy in Jesus' relationship with the Father. That time is identified as being "full of joy through the Holy Spirit" (v. 21). The intimate fellowship that Jesus shared with His Father would now be possible between himself and the disciples through the Holy Spirit.

It would be a blessed *gift*. Luke 11:13 says, "If you then, though you are evil, know how to give good gifts to your children, how much more will your Father in heaven give the Holy Spirit to those who ask him!" Jesus specifically identifies the gift of the Holy Spirit with the gracious act of a loving father. The Holy Spirit is an expression of God's love for us made alive and active throughout the Spirit's presence. He will be a constant and living reminder of God's love.

The coming of the Holy Spirit was so important that Jesus tells His disciples not to go anywhere until He comes. "Stay in Jerusalem and wait," He said. "The Holy Spirit you have heard Me talk about, whom you have seen in My life, will soon fill *you*."

↶ THOUGHTS BEFORE GOD:

Lord, help me wait before You for the Holy Spirit. Help me not be in such a hurry to go places that I miss this special Gift from You. Help me come this week to a new understanding and experience of the Holy Spirit in my life.

✷ PENTECOST—*Acts 1:6-11*

But you will receive power when the Holy Spirit comes on you;
and you will be my witnesses (Acts 1:8).

God gives the Holy Spirit for a purpose. Luke wants us to see and understand this. True, the Holy Spirit comes to be our Comforter and Advocate. He is also our Helper and Friend. Part of the purpose for which God gives the Holy Spirit is His personal ministry to us as individual disciples.

The entire purpose is the accomplishment of the mission Jesus left to His disciples and to us: "You will receive power . . . and you will be my witnesses." Jesus' work was finished. On the hills of Galilee, in the streets of Jerusalem, hanging on the rugged Cross, and standing triumphant over the grave, He did what the Father sent Him to do. The Kingdom was proclaimed and salvation offered. But a great task remained unfinished. The Good News still needed to be carried to the people of Judea and Samaria and beyond, to every corner of the earth.

Entrusted with this monumental task were the same disciples who had so recently demonstrated their faintheartedness and limited understanding of the meaning of Jesus' coming. It is alarming to consider that Jesus was depending on followers who seem disconcertingly like us. What transformed them into the giants of the faith we remember? What gave them the courage and spiritual power to challenge and overcome the mighty Roman Empire?

It was the Holy Spirit. God's work begins with ordinary people as He commissions them with an overwhelming task. They are also given the empowering gift of the Holy Spirit. Luke causes us to view our challenges through the window of Pentecost in the light of the gift of the Holy Spirit. Luke also reminds us that Jesus is coming back at an unknown hour on an unknown day. In the meantime, we have a mission and a Spirit to help us accomplish it.

✷ THOUGHTS BEFORE GOD:

Lord, help me live in the power of the Holy Spirit. Help me be active in doing Your work in the world—not in my strength, but in the power of the Holy Spirit.

ᴄ PENTECOST—Acts 2:1-13

*Suddenly a sound like the blowing of a violent wind
came from heaven. . . . All of them were filled
with the Holy Spirit* (Acts 2:2, 4).

In today's passage we witness one of the most important events of all time. What a scene it must have been to those who were participants in the drama! In one sense it was unique, a once-in-history event. We experience this dimension through the description Luke shares with us. However, in another sense Pentecost is an ongoing event. The Holy Spirit continues to be given to God's people.

One of my favorite stories is that of a famous composer and musician who goes anonymously to visit a church with a renowned pipe organ. As he admires the instrument, its caretaker reacts protectively. When the musician asks to play the organ, the caretaker is reluctant to place the valuable instrument at risk and to surrender his own restrictive authority over it. Finally he relents and allows the organ to be played under his careful supervision. The artist's hands move swiftly and masterfully over the keys. To the humbled caretaker's astonishment, the organ produces a heavenly music that he would have considered beyond the capacity of even this instrument. The echoing melodies and harmonies seemed to open heaven itself. He was transformed by the experience.

When the musician finished, the caretaker lifted a tearstained face to humbly ask the man's name.

"I am Felix Mendelssohn," he said.

On the Day of Pentecost the Holy Spirit demonstrated His transforming mastery. The world would never be the same. And for those of us who follow after, experiencing the power of the Holy Spirit in us, our lives will never be the same either.

ᴄ THOUGHTS BEFORE GOD:

O God, keep me from resisting You. Help me allow the Holy Spirit to freely fill and transform my life.

☙ PENTECOST—*Acts 2:14-21*

And everyone who calls on the name
of the Lord will be saved (Acts 2:21).

The "day of the Lord" (v. 20) had come! This is the message Peter proclaimed at Pentecost. The "day of Yahweh" had been prophesied by the prophet Joel (see Joel 2:28-32). To a people ravaged by a fearsome plague of locusts, Joel preached a word of judgment and promise.

The people of Judah wandered from their covenant relationship with God. They lost their identity as the people of God. They forgot who they were. The results were tragic. They always are. They saw the skies grow dark and their lives ravaged. Their world died.

To these broken people Joel announced the coming of the day of Yahweh. It wasn't ultimately about judgment, but salvation. To people broken and ravaged, Joel said, "God is coming." In that day He will bring salvation and restoration. On that day He will shatter the misery and brokenness of humankind with grace and power. On that day He will seize the flow of history and bend it to His will. On that day He will decisively and powerfully change the human drama forever.

Peter proclaims that day has come! The disciples immediately understood that the coming of the Holy Spirit marked a decisive change in God's presence and work in the world. Neither the disciples nor the world would be the same.

The day of Yahweh had come. God's power and grace were actively and intimately present. The disciples of Jesus Christ in the power of the Holy Spirit would declare the message of hope for the world. "Everyone who calls on the name of the Lord will be saved" (Acts 2:21).

☙ THOUGHTS BEFORE GOD:

Lord, I thank You that the coming of the Holy Spirit has changed my history. Thank You for the transformation of forgiveness and healing and hope. Help me see the troubled events around me in light of Pentecost.

❧ PENTECOST—*Acts 2:22-36*

God has made this Jesus, whom you crucified,
both Lord and Christ (Acts 2:36).

Pentecost is about the coming of the Holy Spirit upon the Church. But the coming of the Holy Spirit was about Jesus Christ. The Holy Spirit does not have a mission separate from the work of Christ. He comes to empower the proclamation of Jesus, to invite us to accept forgiveness through Jesus, to draw us into intimate fellowship with Jesus, and to help us to be made like Jesus.

Peter proclaimed the day of Yahweh, the event that marked God's breaking into history with power. While that day was associated with the advent of the Holy Spirit, Peter immediately identified the event with Jesus Christ. It was the life, death, and resurrection of Jesus that brought the power of God into human history in this decisive way. The Holy Spirit has come for the purpose of empowering the disciples to proclaim that Jesus Christ is Lord.

It is a lesson we need to remember. The Holy Spirit often works in mysterious and dramatic ways. We are naturally inclined to be intrigued by supernatural signs and wonders. We are drawn toward spiritual demonstrations and power. The primary purpose of the Holy Spirit is to lift up Jesus, to draw us to Him to be changed into His likeness. The genuine product of the work of the Holy Spirit is Christlikeness.

Pagan religions have demonstrated spiritual signs and wonders also. Some are as impressive as the miracles in Christian history. What makes our faith wonderfully unique is *Jesus*. So come, Holy Spirit! Fill us with Your presence and power. For through You we come to Jesus Christ, whom God has made both Lord and Christ.

❧ THOUGHTS BEFORE GOD:

May the Holy Spirit be free to work in my life, that through His power the likeness of Christ might be realized and revealed in me.

❧ PENTECOST—*Acts 2:37-47*

When the people heard this, they were cut to the heart. . . .
And the Lord added to their number daily
those who were being saved (Acts 2:37, 47).

Today's passage must be one of the most exciting in the Bible. Pentecost resulted in a Church full of the power and reality of the Holy Spirit, and the people responded dramatically. There was no need for complicated techniques or high-pressure evangelism here. Moved by what they witnessed, spiritually hungry people asked, "What shall we do?" Their hearts were stirred; something within them recognized that here was the answer to their deepest spiritual longings.

Perhaps this is where we should begin our search for renewal and growth in the Church. Programs are good. Contests and promotions can help excite and motivate us. Inspirational speakers and events can challenge us. Organization can help focus our efforts. Good music and good preaching can move us. We should do all of these and more, for the cause of Christ deserves our very best efforts. But at the heart of a church that is really alive we will always find the reality and power of the Holy Spirit.

God gave the Holy Spirit to the Church to help us to accomplish the work of the Kingdom entrusted to us. We can be confident that the Holy Spirit can and will empower the Church to accomplish that commission. The limiting factor in our churches and in our lives is not our resources or abilities. It's not our education or skills. It is the lack of the living empowerment of the Holy Spirit. The story of Acts stands as historical proof of that. The first believers had limited education and skills. They had no marketing training or resources. They had no buildings in strategic locations. They enjoyed no social acceptance. They had no evangelism plan or follow-up organization. All they had was the Holy Spirit working through a receptive and obedient Church.

The story of Pentecost reminds us where we, like the Early Church, need to begin.

❧ THOUGHTS BEFORE GOD:

Lord, help me to begin with You. Help me be open to the work and leading of the Holy Spirit in my life. Send me, use me, and work through me however You choose. Fill me with Your Holy Spirit.

9

ROMANS: THE POWER OF GOD FOR SALVATION

INTRODUCTION

Paul's letter to the Romans outlines the plan and work of salvation. This masterpiece of theology serves as a road map to experiencing and understanding God's will for us concerning our salvation. In it we see the great expanse between what we have been called from and what we have been called to through the grace and power of God in Christ.

QUESTIONS TO THINK ABOUT

What is the wrath of God?

Who can escape the power of sin?

What can overcome the power of sin?

How can we find God in the hard places?

How shall we then live?

❧ ROMANS: THE POWER OF GOD FOR SALVATION
—*Rom. 1:16-17*

I am not ashamed of the gospel,
because it is the power of God for the salvation
of everyone who believes (Rom. 1:16).

All of Paul's letter to the Romans is an expansion and application of what he says in verses 16-17. He begins with a bold declaration that still stirs the hearts of believers. It is easy to imagine Paul dictating this letter as he paces the floor. When he comes to the statement "I am not ashamed of the gospel, because it is the power of God for the salvation of everyone who believes," we picture him with his face set, his voice loudly proclaiming this life-changing truth.

Perhaps thoughts of his own life race through his mind, giving extra meaning to the claim of salvation for *everyone* who believes. Paul keenly remembers his persecution of the followers of Jesus Christ. He recalls the day he held the cloaks for those who stoned Stephen. Deeply aware of his own sinful past, he calls himself "the chief of sinners" (see 1 Timothy 1:15, KJV). But the "everyone" of this passage includes even Paul. Like the words of the old gospel song:

"Whosoever" surely meaneth me.
"Whosoever" meaneth me.
—J. Edwin McConnell

Perhaps Paul reflects on the trials of his faith. He was pursued by those seeking to kill him. The taunts of the crowd, the pain of hurled stones and angry fists, and the hunger and cold endured for the sake of the gospel he proclaimed must have flashed through his mind. Paul's bold and unashamed declaration was no gesture of hollow bravado. It was an expression of faith and courage that would ultimately cost him his life.

It did not matter. What he found was worth the risk—worth the price. He found the power of God that accomplished his salvation. Nothing compared to the worth of that transforming discovery.

❧ THOUGHTS BEFORE GOD:

Lord, thank You for the power of the gospel to save. I am so thankful that Your salvation extends even to me. Thank You for the new life that may be ours through Jesus Christ.

↬ ROMANS: THE POWER OF GOD FOR SALVATION —Rom. 1:18-32

The wrath of God is being revealed from heaven against all the godlessness and wickedness of men (Rom. 1:18).

The wrath of God is one of those challenging biblical concepts that seems so foreign and unpleasant to us. It is easily misunderstood, prone to leave us with an inappropriate, and perhaps damaging, picture of God. This is all the more true because "wrath" presents a ready image to our minds. While it is not a word we commonly use, it conjures up images of intense and destructive anger usually associated with people exercising power to vent that anger. It suggests the image of a God who responds with petulant rage at the disobedience of His subjects.

Such a view powerfully distorts the message of God's wrath here in Romans. God's wrath is not motivated by His anger but is the consequence of our sinful disobedience. It expresses the reality of the harvest that follows the seeding. It is the terrible reality of the destructive nature of sin. It is not about a divine temper tantrum, but a human tragedy of our own creation.

Paul attempts to teach us about the profound consequences of our choices and actions. He helps us to recognize the dark truth—sin destroys. Paul warns us about the terrible results we are preparing for ourselves.

We would like to live in a world without consequences. We would like to imagine we can act in any way we please without responsibility for the disastrous results that follow. Paul is saying we are only trying to kid ourselves. The grim evidence of pain and destruction we see around us is the harvest of our choices and our actions. Our attempt to blame an angry God is only another effort to avoid personal responsibility.

Sin destroys. It will kill you. That's what the wrath of God expresses. Unless we find a remedy, we will surely die at our own hands.

↬ THOUGHTS BEFORE GOD:

Lord, help me recognize the terrible, destructive power of sin. Help me recognize my own responsibility for the choices and actions of my life. Give me the honesty to face the truth of my desperate predicament.

❧ Romans: The Power of God for Salvation
—Rom. 3:21-24

For all have sinned and fall short of the glory of God (Rom. 3:23).

This is one of those statements that doesn't leave any room to run. The "all" is inclusive—none fall outside its claim. We like to think that we are pretty good people. The "bad" folks are somewhere else. *Real* sinners are people who do especially bad things, not the petty crimes of our moral misbehavior.

Paul's statement brings us to an abrupt reality check on two accounts. The first is in our assessment of our lives. The truth is we have an amazing capacity for self-justification and rationalization. I have known people who have committed murder, robbery, physical abuse, and sexual abuse that glibly explain they are not really "bad" people. Circumstances, provocations, and/or mistaken judgments are the extenuating circumstances that excuse or minimize the seriousness of their offenses. Of course, most of us would quickly declare that we do not fall into such a category of offender. Our petty deceits, malice, unfaithfulness, hatred, slander, and selfishness are only minor offenses. Explainable or excusable, they don't really make us *sinners*. Paul challenges us to abandon such self-serving rationalization and to be honest about the serious depth of our moral bankruptcy.

Second, Paul challenges us to be honest about the feeble character of our best and most noble efforts. What appears to be selfless often has only a deeper, more unconventional motivation that remains self-serving. Our best motives are mixed. Our most generous actions are often compromised by self-interest. This doesn't mean we shouldn't affirm them and encourage them. Most emphatically we should. They represent the best of what we are. It's just that the best of what we are is still marked by sin.

The good news is that we can afford to be painfully honest about ourselves because God has provided a remedy. He offers a way to be justified—found truly righteous. So the bad news is that we are universally corrupted by sin. The good news, though, is that we can be justified freely by grace.

❧ Thoughts Before God:

O God, help me be honest before You and with myself. In that painful honesty, help me find the comfort and healing of Your grace.

✌ ROMANS: THE POWER OF GOD FOR SALVATION —Rom. 5:1-11

God demonstrates his own love for us in this:
While we were still sinners, Christ died for us (Rom. 5:8).

If Paul began dictating his letter to the Romans with a set countenance and determined boldness, by now he is pacing the floor in exuberant rejoicing! The grim reality of sin in the human life, the awful consequences that are its sure result, the powerless plight of humankind—they have all been transformed by the loving grace of God. Paul's brutal honesty about our situation is more than matched by the powerful reality of God's grace that has broken into Paul's world and ours.

"Incomprehensible" is a good word to describe the declaration that Christ died for us. That sacrifice was not motivated by an illusion of our worth or virtue. Jesus Christ was painfully aware of the reality of our sin. Yet, knowing us thoroughly, He loved us completely. He paid the price to change our lives. In Him we have peace; we have found our place. We have hope—hope that can overcome the most difficult experiences of life. His death has brought us life. The penalty of the consequences of our sin has been paid. We are free from the judgment of the "wrath" of God.

Charles Wesley expressed the wonder so beautifully:

> *And can it be that I should gain*
> *An int'rest in the Savior's blood?*
> *Died He for me, who caused His pain?*
> *For me who Him to death pursued?*
> *Amazing love! how can it be*
> *That Thou, my God, shouldst die for me?*

Amazing love indeed! It takes broken lives and makes them new. It took *my* broken life and made it new. Small wonder that Paul would be moved to rejoicing—and we with him—at the thought of so great a salvation as this!

✌ THOUGHTS BEFORE GOD:

Lord, I thank You that I may have forgiveness and hope and peace through Christ. I stand amazed at Your great love for me. Thank You for loving me despite my sin and for replacing my burden of sin with a song of joy.

❧ Romans: The Power of God for Salvation —Rom. 8:28-39

And we know that in all things God works for the good
of those who love him (Rom. 8:28).

When Paul spoke the words in today's scripture passage, he lifted us into lofty places. Did he sense the vibrant power of these verses when he first wrote them? He was probably moved to speak from the overflow of his personal experience of the reality of the truth he was proclaiming.

Paul had endured many disappointments, losses, and situations of personal suffering and distress. Many would not consider his life blessed, but it was. We typically associate divine blessings with improved circumstances of life. Such thinking leaves us outside the divine umbrella when we experience loss and brokenness. Paul wants us to know that this gracious power of God for salvation extends beyond the "good times" to redeem and transform *all* times in our lives for good.

God's presence and transforming grace are at work in us and for us even in the worst of situations. Not only on the mountaintop but also in the deepest valley of personal trials and suffering we find God at work. His extraordinary power is revealed in this: No matter the circumstances, He produces good for us if we will let Him. *Nothing* can separate us from the love of God at work in our lives.

Romans 8:28 is not about God causing bad things to happen to us so that good will result. It is about a God who takes the bad, broken, and even the sinful and transforms them miraculously by His grace into good if we will let Him.

Jesus has shown us how far He is willing to go in sharing our experience. Even to the extent of a painful death on a shameful cross, Jesus took our sinful brokenness. Even there He was at work for the good of those who love Him. It is that demonstration that moves Paul to his confidence that no human experience is beyond the transforming grace of God, that nothing can "separate us from the love of God that is in Christ Jesus" (v. 39).

❧ Thoughts Before God:

Lord, thank You for the promise and assurance that there is no place I can go in my life that You cannot transform by Your grace. Thank You that I can know: whatever I experience, I can find You there.

ROMANS: THE POWER OF GOD FOR SALVATION
—*Rom. 12:1-2*

Do not conform any longer to the pattern of this world,
but be transformed by the renewing of your mind (Rom. 12:2).

By the time Paul gets to the end of chapter 11, he is moved to a psalm of praise. Considering the reality of so great a salvation how could he—how could we—not be moved? Despite the cost, God's power is at work for our salvation. We are released from the penalty of sin. Our lives are transformed by His presence and joy. His power to transform extends to *every* experience of life. The psalmist expressed His response so well: "Such knowledge is too wonderful for me, too lofty for me to attain" (Ps. 139:6).

Paul doesn't expect to comprehend this loving redemption, but to respond to it. Faced with the reality and power of God's work of salvation for us, how can we do less than offer ourselves to God? "Living sacrifices" (Rom. 12:1) is the image Paul uses. He calls us to surrender our lives to God. No longer are we given to the world and dominated by the sin that destroys us, but we're transformed into the image of the One who loves and redeems us.

We are granted not only escape from death, but also the experience of new life. Paul knows that the world will relentlessly attempt to reshape our lives into its own image. In the workplace, in the marketplace, in the popular media, and in the culture of our communities, the world will call, prod, threaten, and squeeze us into its mold. But we realize that the result is brokenness and death. The call of the world beckons us to destruction with a pleasing and persistent song. God invites us to be shaped by a different calling, to be remade according to His pattern.

The power of God for our salvation takes us from brokenness and death into the experience of new and transformed life in Jesus Christ. It is no wonder that Paul could boldly declare, "I am not ashamed of the gospel, because it is the power of God for the salvation of everyone who believes" (Rom. 1:16).

THOUGHTS BEFORE GOD:

Lord, help me stand boldly with Paul, unashamed of the gospel of Jesus Christ, which saves and transforms my life. Lord, my life is Yours to remold and use. Let the power of salvation be revealed and demonstrated in my life—for Your glory.

10

PHILIPPIANS: LIFE IN CHRIST

INTRODUCTION

Paul's New Testament letter to the Philippians focuses on the person and work of Christ. It is a call to life centered on Christ and lived in Him. He is the model for the life we should lead and the goal toward which we should strive.

QUESTIONS TO THINK ABOUT

What is the secret Paul has found?
What is the standard by which we should measure our lives?
What does Paul value above everything else?
How is the runner a model for the Christian life?
What is the secret of learning contentment?

↬ PHILIPPIANS: LIFE IN CHRIST—*Phil. 1:3-11*

He who began a good work in you
will carry it on to completion (Phil. 1:6).

God is not finished with you yet." That seems to be the message Paul is expressing to the Philippians as he begins his letter to them. Not a threat or an ominous beginning, Paul's appreciation and affection for the Philippians shows through from his first address: "I thank my God every time I remember you" (v. 3). What a wonderful commentary on the Philippians and their relationship with Paul!

The message of God's unfinished business is a positive one. It is a message of encouragement and challenge. It offers encouragement because it promises that God will complete what He has begun. We are usually not so reliable. We begin something with the best of intentions. Then we get bored or distracted, and the endeavor is forgotten. But God doesn't forget. He doesn't get distracted. What He has begun in us will not get lost along the way. He is in it for the long haul—all the way, no matter what.

The message of unfinished business is also a challenge Paul wants to pass along to the Philippians and to us. As thankful as he is for what they have done and how far they have come, Paul wants more for them. His prayer for the abounding of their love, knowledge, understanding, and discernment suggests some areas of growth that Paul wants them to experience. God isn't finished yet. He has more for them.

The challenge to the Philippians is not prompted by God's displeasure with them. Neither is God's challenge to us. Rather, it is the loving invitation of a Father to His children to the best He can offer. It is not about our falling short, but about His offering more. This word about God's unfinished business is good news.

↬ THOUGHTS BEFORE GOD:

Lord, thank You for the news that You are not finished yet. Thank You for the encouragement that You will see me through this journey, no matter what may come. Thank You for the good news that there are even better things in store for me. Help me walk confidently and obediently into my future with You.

❧ Philippians: Life in Christ—*Phil. 1:20-26*

For to me, to live is Christ and to die is gain (Phil. 1:21).

Paul begins the heart of his letter by placing his own life in perspective. He is in chains, imprisoned for the sake of the gospel. While he hopes to win release, his life is in peril. Paul writes in the shadow of a martyr's death that will eventually be his fate. At the same time, there are those in the church who are taking advantage of his misfortune. A more difficult position can scarcely be imagined. Yet Paul is at peace. He has found the secret to a victorious life.

Paul's secret is a life focused and centered on Jesus Christ. The service of Christ is his purpose. Fellowship with Christ is his goal. Roman chains can rob him of physical liberty, but not spiritual triumph. To serve Christ, even in imprisonment or persecution, is Paul's greatest aspiration. To be ushered into Christ's presence, even by means of a Roman execution, would be his highest blessing. The Christ-centered focus of Paul's life disarms the Romans. They cannot deprive Paul of his deepest desires. His peace is beyond their reach.

Paul demonstrates in his own life the secret for completing the work God has begun in us. When our lives are centered on Christ, our meaning found in Him, our fulfillment attained in Him, we stand beyond the reach of the world. The misfortunes and injustices of life are real to us; we hurt like everyone else. But those "slings and arrows of outrageous fortune" cannot reach far enough to upset the balance of our lives. They cannot rob us of our peace or hope.

The liberating power of life in Christ is not spiritual escapism from the world. In fact, it enables us to live boldly. Paul can accept the challenge of living under difficult circumstances for the sake of the Philippians and the Church because his life is in Christ. We, too, can face the difficulties and disappointments of life boldly and courageously. For life at its worst cannot take away our life at its best. "For to me, to live is Christ and to die is gain" (v. 21).

❧ Thoughts Before God:

Lord, help me find my life in You. In the middle of life's struggles, help me keep focused on You. Be the Center of all my life.

✧ PHILIPPIANS: LIFE IN CHRIST—*Phil. 2:1-11*

*Your attitude should be the same
as that of Christ Jesus* (Phil. 2:5).

Today's scripture reading is one of the great passages of the New Testament. It includes the majestic Christ hymn of verses 6-11. Paul uses it in presenting a model for the Christian life.

It is a radically different perspective for life than the one we see modeled in the world around us. We learn early in life that our key to happiness and success is learning to get the world to serve us. We learn we can get food or attention if we cry. As we grow older, we become more sophisticated about our methods, but the strategy is still the same: the world has what we want or need—how can we get it?

In contrast, Paul offers the example of Christ. It moves in a completely different direction.

Jesus is the Son of God. We can hardly begin to imagine what that means. The most privileged royalty in the world is only a shadow of His majesty and power. He would never have to suffer want, pain, loss, discomfort, or weakness. Yet He chose, out of love for us, to relinquish all of that and "emptied" himself. He gave up His place as Son of God to take the place of a servant. "Nothing" (v. 7), Paul calls it. Broken. Powerless. Empty.

In that emptying of himself, Jesus became a man. He took on humanity with all the limitations, deprivations, and suffering that are a part of fleshly existence. The One who could command legions of angels now assumes the role of a humbly obedient servant. The One who is Life itself now subjects himself to death.

Jesus Christ, who had the right and ability to make the world serve Him, chose instead to give himself for the sake of the world. That, Paul says, is a model worth following.

Make Christ's attitude your attitude. Let His example be your guide as you make decisions about how you will live. The measure of our lives as Christians is to be a reflection of Christ.

✧ THOUGHTS BEFORE GOD:

O God, help me be like Christ. Forgive me for my self-centeredness. Let Christ change my heart and direct my life.

❧ PHILIPPIANS: LIFE IN CHRIST—*Phil. 3:1-11*

I consider everything a loss compared to the
surpassing greatness of knowing Christ (Phil. 3:8).

Some people think the goal of the Christian life is to be religious. We learn the language of the Church. We know the hymns and we know the rules. We're at home in the Church culture. We even look and dress as though we're pious. So we must be holy. Right?

Paul knew people who thought like that. They took great pride in their religious virtue. Perhaps we know some folks like that. Perhaps we tend to be like that ourselves. If so, we ought to be concerned. Paul makes it absolutely clear that such people have missed the point.

The point is Jesus Christ. Our faith isn't focused on our heritage or external signs of piety. Our efforts shouldn't be directed toward being more religious than anyone else and certainly not toward just looking more religious. Paul, who had as much right as anyone to be proud of his religious pedigree, calls it rubbish in comparison with something far more significant. That something is knowing Christ.

Paul doesn't mean just knowing who Jesus is or having information about Him. He's talking about an intimate, personal relationship. Paul has a deep longing for Christ. The psalmist expressed a similar feeling when he wrote, "As the deer pants for streams of water, so my soul pants for you, O God. My soul thirsts for God, for the living God" (Ps. 42:1-2). No other goal moves Paul like that of knowing Christ.

Paul points us to a level of spiritual life that most of us are still working toward. More than anything else, he is moved by the prospect of experiencing Christ more fully, more intimately. His motivations have been refined until it is the desire to know Christ that moves him more than anything else. God is not finished with us until we, too, can say from the deepest part of ourselves, "I want to know Christ" (Phil. 3:10).

❧ THOUGHTS BEFORE GOD:

Lord, please cultivate in me the kind of deep longing and desire for You that Paul expressed. Finish Your work in me until I long above all else for Christ alone.

PHILIPPIANS: LIFE IN CHRIST—*Phil. 3:12-16*

One thing I do: Forgetting what is behind
and straining toward what is ahead,
I press on toward the goal (Phil. 3:13-14).

Having declared that Christ is the goal of his life, Paul goes on to describe what a life focused on that goal looks like. It is not that we have achieved the goal. It is not that we are already perfect and our spiritual journey completed. Perfect accomplishment is not the standard that Paul claims for himself or proposes for us.

The image Paul describes is that of an athletic model. It is the picture of the runner whose every effort and attention is focused on the successful completion of the race. Absent from his mind are thoughts of yesterday's activities or tomorrow's plans. No physical effort is expended on any purpose other than running the race. His mind, heart, and body are totally invested in the goal before him. All else fades in significance for the sake of the prize he runs to win.

It is this image that Paul suggests as the picture of the Christian life. It is a life totally given to serve Christ and to know Him. No other values or goals in life compare to the worth of this surpassing prize. Left behind are self-serving ambitions. Abandoned are distracting or destructive habits of life. Our energies and desires are focused. Our will is ordered by this one thing.

Paul recognizes that the danger threatening the Philippians is not abandonment of God, but halfhearted pursuit of God. The besetting temptation of our lives is spiritual mediocrity or perpetual immaturity. We settle for the adequate. We are satisfied by the superficial.

Don't settle for anything less than all God has for you, Paul says. The prize is worth running the race. Press on with a single-minded focus to reach for "the prize for which God [calls us] . . . in Christ Jesus" (v. 14).

THOUGHTS BEFORE GOD:

Lord, help me desire You above all else. Let all other things in life find their priorities behind this one thing—to know and serve You.

✷ PHILIPPIANS: LIFE IN CHRIST—*Phil. 4:10-13*

I have learned the secret of being content. . . .
I can do everything through him
who gives me strength (Phil. 4:12-13).

In life in Christ Paul has discovered the secret to that most rare of human conditions: contentment. It is more difficult to attain than wealth or fame or power. It is an elusive prize. The rich and powerful cannot find it any more easily than can the poor and powerless. Yet it is a necessary component of the truly happy life. It is the crowning evidence of true success. And Paul has found the secret.

That secret is simply the realization and acceptance that Jesus is all I need. Not Jesus *and,* but Jesus *alone.* Contentment is the state in which we are able to say, "I lack nothing that is necessary for my happiness and well-being."

We must come to the place where we accept what we have as adequate. No matter our circumstances, we accept by faith that we already have in Christ all we need to be content. Paul had found this to be true. In unbearable circumstances, Paul experienced contentment. This liberating truth sets us free from discontentment regarding our finances, career, marriage, or health. In *all* things we may experience contentment.

It is difficult to explain exactly how it works—that in difficult, discouraging, or painful circumstances we may still have contentment. But it is true. Perhaps it is that Jesus himself is always to be found there. He comforts us and satisfies us. He fills the empty places with himself. In a miraculous way we find contentment—in Him. God is not finished with you yet, Paul writes to the Philippians. But He will make the journey with you, and He will lead you into wonderful and pleasant places. Don't miss the rest of the journey.

✷ THOUGHTS BEFORE GOD:

Lord, help me find contentment in You. Help me stop looking to things and people to fill my empty places. Become the secret of my contentment. Help me find You, and having found You, know that I have found all I need.

11

FIRST JOHN: REAL LIFE WITH CHRIST

INTRODUCTION

John's letter addresses an old problem that is still around: how important is my everyday lifestyle to my spiritual life? John gives a clear and uncompromising answer: What I believe and how I live are two parts of the same faith walk.

QUESTIONS TO THINK ABOUT

What does it mean to me that Jesus came in the flesh? Why is that important?

How does John give us a realistic, yet redemptive, understanding of sin?

Can I live a sinful life and still be born of God?

What does my relationship with God have to do with my relationships with other people?

How does God's plan for me include eternity *and* real life right now?

☙ 1 JOHN: REAL LIFE WITH CHRIST—*1 John 1:1-4*

We write this to make our joy complete (1 John 1:4).

J ohn writes his first letter to confront an old problem. It was making the rounds when John wrote the letter, and it is still around today. It is the idea that Christian faith is a spiritual concern somehow disconnected from real life—the idea that as long as our spirit life is OK, our worldly actions, involvement, and relationships aren't really that important.

From the very beginning of this letter, John wants to let us know what he thinks and God thinks about ideas like these. The Eternal God—the Word of Life, the One who was before all things—is the One whom John has seen with human eyes and touched with human hands. This One walked and talked and laughed and cried and hurt and died—in the flesh. He left heaven to experience hunger and pain, because He wanted to have fellowship, a relationship with people.

God considered the lives of human persons in the flesh so important that He gave himself to become a part of human life. He brings to mind a story about a little girl. She was afraid and unwilling to sleep alone in her bedroom one night because of a loud thunderstorm. Her father tried to comfort her. He assured her that she was safe, and he tried to remind her of God's care. He asked her if she remembered that God loved her.

She did, she replied, but she needed some love "with skin on."

John is reminding us that our faith is about "love with skin on." We don't believe in a disconnected, spiritualized faith. Jesus himself has shown us that what happens in real life with real people *really* matters.

☙ THOUGHTS BEFORE GOD:

Lord, help me remember that what I do today and the people I meet really matter to You. You cared enough to live in my world. Help me live for You in my world.

1 John: Real Life with Christ
—1 John 1:5—2:2

*If we confess our sins, he is faithful and just
and will forgive us our sins and purify us
from all unrighteousness (1 John 1:9).*

What are you going to do with sin? That's the problem John confronted as he began his letter. That question still demands an answer. The response popular in John's day, and still popular in ours, was, and is, to deny its reality. The false teaching John was writing against suggested that sin had to do with the fleshly, material life and not with spiritual people like themselves. Common bodily actions didn't have any effect on their spiritual security and status. Real life, everyday life in this world with flesh and blood people, really didn't matter, according to this teaching. Doing the right things, acting in the right ways, living a holy life "with skin on" was disconnected from the question of our "spiritual" status. In reply, John emphasizes very clearly three things about sin.

Sin is real. You can't pretend or explain it away. If you do, you are just lying to yourself. The "ostrich" strategy of trying to get rid of a problem by not seeing it won't solve the problem. In John's world (and ours) there were lots of people who wanted to deal with the problem of sin by pretending it was not there.

Sin is unacceptable to God. Our God is not disconnected from the material world. He is very much concerned about how we live real life. If we pretend that God cares only about our spiritual status, then we are fooling ourselves. Having (spiritual) fellowship with God and living a sinful life is not an option.

Sin has a remedy. It's easy to understand people who want to deny sin's reality. In our own resources we can do little to fix the problem of sin. If our own resources were all we had, the "ostrich" strategy might be a good choice. But the good news is we have a resource with which to deal with sin. We don't have to live in denial of sin's reality. We have this unqualified promise: "If we confess our sins, he is faithful and just and will forgive us our sins and purify us from all unrighteousness" (1:9). Sin is a problem God can handle.

⤳ THOUGHTS BEFORE GOD:

Lord, help me be honest before You. Because of Your grace and love, I don't have to hide from the reality of my sins. When I fall short, I can turn to You. Help me do that.

❧ 1 John: Real Life with Christ—*1 John 3:7-10*

No one who is born of God will continue to sin. . . .
he cannot go on sinning,
because he has been born of God (1 John 3:9).

When we talk about what it means to be a Christian, what we believe and how we live together, John wants us to understand that spiritual faith and real (bodily) life are not separate issues as far as God is concerned. If we believe and are born of God by faith, our lives will show it.

That doesn't mean that our lives will be a perfect reflection of the faith we profess. We are still imperfect human persons, and we will be until we are transformed in eternity. John makes an important and very helpful distinction in this letter. He distinguishes between two lifestyles. The first is one that is fundamentally committed to following Christ. In this life there may be instances of sin or falling short of the goal of perfectly following Christ. But these are "exceptions to the rule" in a life that reflects the transforming work of God. The second lifestyle is one of "sinning" or ongoing sinful behavior, that is, the life of a person who chooses a lifestyle of continuing sin. Here willful sin is an accepted pattern, the "rule."

John wants his readers to understand that when we experience occasions of falling short of the goal, the grace of Christ is a ready remedy (see 2:1-2). However, that free grace does not extend to a lifestyle of continuing sin, unrepented and unchanged. The grace of Christ is not a safety net for people who live lives of willful, ongoing sin.

If we are in relationship with Christ as a child of God, then that relationship will be reflected in how we live our lives. How could it not? It may be reflected imperfectly; my life may have major areas that still need changing—but I am a work of transformation "in progress."

Coming into relationship with Christ involves repentance, a willful turning away from sin. A life that reflects a pattern of sinning has not yet turned away from sin. That life has not been born of God. It is still being lived under the lordship of the evil one.

❧ Thoughts Before God:

Lord, change me. Let my life reflect Your love and righteousness. Don't let me try to justify my sin, but rather, help me repent and turn from it. Be Lord of all my life.

1 JOHN: REAL LIFE WITH CHRIST—*1 John 3:13-18*

This is how we know what love is: Jesus Christ laid down
his life for us. And we ought to lay down
our lives for our brothers (1 John 3:16).

A life lived in Jesus Christ will show it. How we live will reflect what we believe and whom we follow. That is true not only for our personal moral behavior but for our relationships with others as well. How we live in real life with real people matters to God. It mattered enough to Him to become one like us and to live among us. He showed us that it was important to Him. And He showed us how He wants us to live with each other.

Live as Jesus lived; love as Jesus loved. That's the message and the challenge. That principle will change how I relate to other people. It will change how I act toward them. To love them is not to have warm feelings, but to act for their good. If I have what a brother or sister needs and I withhold it, how can I say that I really love him or her? How I spend my material resources and how I expend my energies and talents will be affected by the love God produces in me for my brother. That doesn't mean we automatically sell all we have and give it away. But it does mean that loving others as Jesus loves places a claim on what we have.

When I was a child, I claimed all I could see as my own. When I became an adult, my world came to include my family and friends. Jesus wants me to include the unknown "other" in my world, as He did in His. If I do, that will necessarily change how I spend my money, use my influence, think about race and class, and respond to the unattractive and needy. My life will be different because Jesus has brought other people into it. It will be no longer just "Jesus and me," but Jesus and me and other people whom Jesus loves and wants me to love.

Learning to live this way is not so much a destination as it is a journey. I will never completely arrive, but John makes it abundantly clear that I need to be on my way. Being "on the way" is one of the marks of those who follow Jesus.

✎ THOUGHTS BEFORE GOD:

Lord, help me love as You love. Teach me to see others as You see them. Help me learn new attitudes and act in new ways. Help me spend my resources and time—myself—in ways that reflect You in my life.

➤ 1 JOHN: REAL LIFE WITH CHRIST—*1 John 4:7-19*

There is no fear in love.
But perfect love drives out fear (1 John 4:18).

Today's focal verse, 1 John 4:18, is one of the profound insights of 1 John. It tells us one of the logical implications of understanding God. John is an avid logician. His writing is full of either-or arguments and "if . . . then" statements (that is, if one thing is true, then another truth follows from that). For most of us, that kind of exercise in logic has very limited appeal, but the lessons John teaches us through it have great importance.

John begins with the understanding of a God who is eternal Spirit and absolute Creator. But this God is also infinitely loving and cares about humans and human life. He cares so much that God's own and only Son is sent to share human life to redeem human persons. In fact, the Son enters fully into the human experience, even suffering a terrible death. All this takes place because God cares so deeply and passionately about us—He loves us.

God's kind of love is not a "using" kind of love, in which He desires us because it serves His needs. It's not even a mutual kind of love, in which both parties bring something to the relationship in a kind of partnership and exchange. It's a kind of love that God shows us in Jesus Christ. It's a selfless, giving love that acts in response to the other's needs. It's gracious, and it loves despite any unloveliness in the one loved. It's an extraordinary, marvelous, divine kind of love.

The lesson, then, is that if God is a God who loves like that and if He is the God I am trying to follow, then why would I ever need to be afraid of Him? What is there in His character to fear? What caprice or cruelty or harshness can I expect from Him? If I can learn to understand God's perfect love, then I will never be afraid of Him again.

Our problem is that we project human love or other characteristics onto God. We see God like a demanding earthly parent. We picture

Him with the face of some harsh authority figure who scarred our lives. We imagine that God loves as we love.

But He's not like that. John wants us to know this—because really knowing it can set us free.

↷ THOUGHTS BEFORE GOD:

Lord, teach me to really understand Your kind of love. Forgive me for picturing You in ways that are false. Let me grasp Your perfect love so completely that there is no room left for fear.

❧ 1 JOHN: REAL LIFE WITH CHRIST
—1 John 5:11-12, 18-21

God has given us eternal life, and this life is in his Son. . . .
Dear children, keep yourselves from idols (1 John 5:11, 21).

The end of a letter is a good place to find a brief statement of the things that are really important to the writer. John ends his letter trying to get his message through. In this we see the issues that are closest to his heart.

The heart of John's message is in verses 11 and 12. God has given us eternal life in Jesus Christ, His Son. Eternal life *beyond* this existence in the flesh has come to us *through* life in the flesh, the life of Jesus. What happens in this fleshly life matters beyond it. It matters to God, and it should matter to us. In fact, eternal life comes *only* through the Son, who came in the flesh. Either eternal life comes through a relationship with the "Word made flesh" (see John 1:14, KJV), or it doesn't come at all—period.

John reminds us in verse 18 that a relationship with a God who came in the flesh is a transforming faith lived out in the flesh. Our lives are changed. We live differently. Our spiritual transformation is reflected in how we live "real life." The world reflects the rule of the evil one. Followers of Jesus Christ reflect *His* rule.

At first glance it seems John's closing remark about idols is out of place. He hasn't talked about idols at all in this letter. Or has he? An idol is something in which we place our faith. We put confidence in it and guide our lives by it. Trust in a spiritualized faith disconnected from real life is an idol. John is saying, "Don't entrust yourself to idols like that." Life is to be found only in Jesus Christ, who lived real life in the flesh and wants to change our lives in the flesh too. Our God is a God who transforms us into His image. Any other god is an idol.

❧ THOUGHTS BEFORE GOD:

Lord, live in me. Change my life in every part. Make my faith in You the guiding and transforming center of who I am and how I live. In my life, Lord, be glorified.

REVELATION: THE END OF THE STORY

INTRODUCTION

This week we look at the end of time, the end of the story. Given to a church struggling with discouragement and persecution, Revelation brings us a message of encouragement and hope. It helps us to keep our lives and our experiences in the right perspective—the perspective we get by looking at the end of the story.

QUESTIONS TO THINK ABOUT

What is the Revelation really about? How should I understand it?

How does the vision of the end of the story change how I see the world I live in every day?

How is my life similar to the experience of the Church at the end of the first century?

What is the message of Revelation for me?

✤ REVELATION: THE END OF THE STORY—*Rev. 1:1-3*

*Blessed are those who hear it [this prophecy] and take to heart
what is written in it, because the time is near (Rev. 1:3).*

Revelation is a curious book. It is full of strange creatures, fantastic places, and terrible scenes. It is full of symbolic language and numbers and obscure, often frightening, images. Often we tend to leave Revelation to those interested in interpreting events and anticipating the future. Many avoid Revelation because they find it confusing or disturbing. That's unfortunate, because the Book of Revelation contains such a universal message of encouragement.

The Revelation was given to a church in distress. Many years had passed since Jesus ascended into heaven with the promise of His return. One by one the apostles had been martyred. Perhaps only John remained of those who had walked and talked with Jesus. Was Jesus ever to return? Did we misunderstand? Was our faith misplaced after all? With each passing year the questions grew louder and more insistent.

To make matters worse, the Roman authorities were increasing the persecution of Christians. Misunderstood, sometimes feared, the members of this obscure religious sect were easy targets for those anxious for a scapegoat or victim. Believers would gather in uncertainty and sometimes fear. The future of the Christian Church seemed awfully bleak. Were they seeing the end of those who followed Jesus? The prospects certainly did not look very good.

It was to this church that the Revelation was given. To those who were discouraged or afraid, it was a reminder that God was still at work on their behalf. It was a glimpse beyond the apparent reality of the Church's defeat to the *ultimate* reality of God's absolute triumph. We may be down, but we're not out. We may be hard pressed, but we're not defeated. Revelation reminds us that beyond what we can see, God controls the end of the story.

✤ THOUGHTS BEFORE GOD:

Lord, help me hear the promise and receive Your encouragement. You have not forgotten. You are not absent. And just as You control the end of the story of history, You hold the end of my story in Your hands too. That's good news. Thank You.

Then I saw a Lamb, looking as if it had been slain,
standing in the center of the throne (Rev. 5:6).

Revelation is a book of pictures. It contains a series of visual images that portray the power and meaning of "the end of the story." To understand it and appreciate its impact, we need to "see" it. As you glimpse these scenes, try to place yourself into the picture. See the beauty. Feel the power.

This scene places us before the throne of God, the center of all power, truth, and holiness. Chapter 4 describes its strange and awesome beauty. Simply to be there is to be overcome with God's presence. In God's hand is a scroll, sealed with seven seals. This scroll holds the unfolding of God's plan for human history. Sealed within it is His plan for our redemption and restoration. It holds all our hope. The scroll will not only tell the story but also release its fulfillment. It contains the answer to our desperate plight.

The call goes out for one who is worthy to break the seals and open the scroll, releasing God's work of redemption. Silently we wait, looking for someone to open the scroll. But there is no one. No one in heaven or on earth or under the earth is worthy—no one. John wept. We should weep too. All our hope is sealed in the unbroken scroll. We are helpless, left hopeless.

No—wait! Look! There *is* One who can open the scroll. Now we see Him, a Lamb. What a curious figure to be the key to human history! Not only is He a Lamb, but His body bears the marks of one slain. He is as one wounded, even dead. This One, and this One alone, is worthy to open the scroll. Wounded for me—yes, wounded for me! He comes and takes the scroll into His marked hand. All our hope and all our despair are held in the grasp of the wounded Lamb.

Little wonder, then, that heaven echoes with the songs of praise and worship. The Lamb is worthy. He comes to save us!

❧ THOUGHTS BEFORE GOD:

Thank You for the Lamb. I was lost before You came for me, hopeless before you redeemed me. By Your stripes I am healed. Help me truly worship You today. You have replaced my weeping with joy.

These are they who have come out of the great tribulation. . . . And God will wipe away every tear from their eyes (Rev. 7:14, 17).

Remember the audience. Remember the church to whom the Revelation is given—a persecuted minority, a battered band of weary pilgrims. They know about tribulation. They know about suffering. They know about fear. They know about tears. What they don't know is where this trail of tears is leading them. So God shows them.

To Christians gathered in small groups, perhaps in secret or in hiding, the curtain draws back to reveal this scene. As far as the eye can see, farther than our ability to count, the multitude of God's children are gathered together. No quiet prayer meeting here! No subdued whispers—the choruses of praise echo loudly.

What a scene! It is greater than the grandest spectacles of Rome. How different from the present experience of these battle-weary Christians! How wonderful it would be to be in *that* assembly! Who could these people be? What noble nation, what victorious heritage are they privileged to claim as their own?

"These are they who have come out of the great tribulation; they have washed their robes and made them white in the blood of the Lamb" (v. 14). In other words, they are who *you* will be. These days of persecution and sorrow will quickly pass. The days of rejoicing will be forever. For a time you may seem alone. For all time you will be in this great multitude. Now you may cry. In that day He, the Lamb, will wipe away every tear. I can imagine tears of hope and joy as the Revelation is read to weary disciples. The dark and hidden meeting places will be transformed by the vision of that great day.

Remember the audience. The Revelation is given to those who are wounded and discouraged, weary pilgrims on the way. Not all of those people lived in the first century. Some of them may be reading these lines. The vision is for us too. When the days seem long and the battle hard, remember this scene.

↦ THOUGHTS BEFORE GOD:

Thank You, Lord, for drawing back the curtain to allow us to see this scene at the end of the story. My troubles are not the end. Your victory is.

↫ REVELATION: THE END OF THE STORY
—Rev. 13:11—14:5

He [the beast] also forced everyone . . . to receive a mark. . . .
Then I looked, and there before me was the Lamb . . .
and with him 144,000 who had his name and
his Father's name written on their foreheads (Rev. 13:16; 14:1).

This is one of those texts that has a great deal in it beyond my understanding. Wiser people than I will have to decipher it (many have tried for centuries with limited success). But there is a simple message in this story that is clear, even to me. It becomes obvious when we run chapters 13 and 14 together. (Sometimes it helps to remember that the chapter and verse divisions weren't in the original text.)

We are witnessing a great struggle for the earth and the people who live on it. Evil emerges incarnate in the person of the beast in Rev. 13:11. The text we are considering today tells the story of two groups of people and the two different signs they wear. The sign is more than a physical mark. It isn't an accident. It tells who they are, where their allegiance and loyalties lie. Some bear the mark of the beast, and their lives reflect his lordship. Others bear the name of the Lamb, and their lives reflect His lordship—"they are blameless" (14:5).

The real point of this contrast is to remind us that we will wear a mark on our lives. Our lives will reflect our discipleship of Jesus Christ and His Lordship, or they will reflect our own sovereignty and the lordship of the evil one. It's not about hidden codes on your social security card or banking plan. It's about the name written on the forehead and hands of your life.

Revelation 13:17 says that no one could buy or sell without the mark of the beast. The world tells us that we will fail without compromise. You must bend your ethics and "get a little dirty" to get by. Do you want to be popular? Do you want to be successful? Just let your life reflect the mark. Cooperate with "the program."

Revelation reminds the battle-weary disciples of the first century—and every century—that there is another option. Not everyone accepts the mark. Some choose to have the name of the Lamb written boldly and publicly upon the "foreheads" of their lives. Some still say, "I have decided to follow Jesus," and let their lives reveal Christ. Like the first-century audience who first heard the Revelation, we have a choice to make. Which sign will my life bear?

↶ THOUGHTS BEFORE GOD:

Lord, help me wear Your name boldly in my life. Help me resist the temptations to bear the world's mark, no matter the price. "I have decided to follow Jesus; / No turning back, no turning back" (Anonymous).

❧ Revelation: The End of the Story —Rev. 19:11-21

I saw heaven standing open and there before me was
a white horse, whose rider is called Faithful and True. . . .
On his robe and on his thigh he has this name written:
KING OF KINGS AND LORD OF LORDS (Rev. 19:11, 16).

What a scene! In chapter 18 the fall of Babylon is graphically described. The kingdom of worldly power lies in smoldering ruins. The first-century audience of the Revelation could hardly have failed to see the fall of Rome in this picture. For them, the Roman Empire embodied earthly power and evil. Revelation displays to embattled Christians the total devastation of their oppressor.

Chapter 19 begins with echoes of praise and celebration from a numberless multitude, declaring the glory of God and the victory of the Lamb. Then we see it. The sky opens like a great dome, more vast than we can imagine. And through the opening comes a white horse, striking in its beauty and strength. Astride the horse, with eyes like fire and filled with majesty, we see Him. Even without the name written on His robe and thigh we would know Him. He is the "KING OF KINGS AND LORD OF LORDS." He is the Lamb, slain but victorious. He is our Lord.

Behind Him, as far as the eye can see, are the armies of heaven. Beyond our ability to count, awesome in their splendor and dignity, they fill the sky as they come to our aid. In that moment weary warriors are refreshed. Discouraged disciples are heartened. These are the resources of heaven that do battle for us. Here is where the victory rests. Can you envision the power of this scene for those battle-weary Christians of the first century?

Sometimes I feel a little battle weary myself. Sometimes I feel discouraged. Sometimes I am overwhelmed at the size of the challenge and the limits of my resources. In those times I like to think about this scene at the end of the story. In the light of this vision, even my greatest struggles are no longer overwhelming, the battle no longer seems so uncertain. One day the sky will open, and we will see Him.

❧ Thoughts Before God:

Lord, lift my eyes above the struggles to see You. Help me live in the encouragement and power of this great day that is surely coming. Help me remember the end of the story.

❧ REVELATION: THE END OF THE STORY—*Rev. 21:1-5*

He who was seated on the throne said,
"I am making everything new!" (Rev. 21:5).

The Revelation is about the end of the story. It's about the One who is finally in control. It's about Him who is really winning this battle that is raging around us. To the Church at the end of the first century, "the end of the story" was beginning to look pretty clear—and it wasn't good news.

The Revelation is God's reminder to us that things are not always as they seem. We live in a world where the enemy has the power of appearance. Wrong appears more attractive, more exciting, and more powerful. We are too easily deceived into believing what we see.

The world around us is not the end of the story. When we see sin applauded, corruption rewarded, and virtue punished, we are seeing only part of the picture. When we see the strength of the enemy and our own limits and meager resources, we are witnessing only part of the story.

John's revelation draws back the curtain of history to show us what is real. It's not about fantasies or wishful dreams. It is a true portrayal of what *will* be. It allows us to truly see the end of the story.

God is making everything new. This world's fading glory and self-destructive behaviors will not be the final chapter to the history of the human race. God's hand holds the scroll. Christ's coming changes the story—and its ending.

Revelation tells us to take heart. Don't be discouraged or defeated. Don't be misled by the enemy's apparent strength or seeming victory. *God is in control of the story's ending!*

❧ THOUGHTS BEFORE GOD:

Thank You, Lord, for the Revelation You gave John to share with us. Help me remember that You are in control. Help me to live looking beyond the appearances around me. Help me instead to live boldly in hope, confident that the end of the story is in Your hands.